AF386479

Empire Ablaze

Empire Ablaze

The American Revolution and the Atlantic Working Class

Tom Cutterham

VERSO
London • New York

First published by Verso 2026

The manufacturer's authorized representative in the EU for product safety (GPSR)
is LOGOS EUROPE, 9 rue Nicolas Poussin, 17000, La Rochelle, France
contact@logoseurope.eu

1 3 5 7 9 10 8 6 4 2

Verso
UK: 6 Meard Street, London W1F 0EG
US: 207 East 32nd Street, New York, NY 10016
versobooks.com

Verso is the imprint of New Left Books

ISBN-13: 978-1-83674-145-9
ISBN-13: 978-1-83674-147-3 (UK EBK)
ISBN-13: 978-1-83674-148-0 (US EBK)

British Library Cataloguing in Publication Data
A catalogue record for this book is available from the British Library

Library of Congress Cataloging-in-Publication Data

Names: Cutterham, Tom, 1987- author
Title: Empire ablaze : the American Revolution and the Atlantic working
  class / Tom Cutterham.
Description: London : Verso, 2026. | Includes bibliographical references
  and index.
Identifiers: LCCN 2026009863 (print) | LCCN 2026009864 (ebook) | ISBN
  9781836741459 hardback | ISBN 9781836741480 ebook
Subjects: LCSH: Aitken, James, 1752-1777 | United
  States—History—Revolution, 1775-1783—Underground movements | United
  States—History—Revolution, 1775-1783—Influence | Navy-yards and naval
  stations—England—Portsmouth—History—18th century |
  Harbors—England—Bristol—History—18th century | Great
  Britain—Colonies—Administration—Corrupt practices | Radicalism—Great
  Britain—History—18th century | Working class—Political
  activity—History—18th century | LCGFT: Biographies
Classification: LCC E280.A49 C87 2026 (print) | LCC E280.A49 (ebook)
LC record available at https://lccn.loc.gov/2026009863
LC ebook record available at https://lccn.loc.gov/2026009864

Typeset in Minion by Hewer Text UK Ltd, Edinburgh
Printed and bound by CPI Group (UK) Ltd, Croydon CR0 4YY

Contents

James Aitken, Alias John the Painter, 1777 (John Carter
Brown Library, Archive of Early American Images)

Introduction

'Remember John the Painter', wrote an anonymous New Jersey revolutionary in the summer of 1780. 'He was a poor man', utterly lacking in the usual forms of power: wealth or status, friends in high places, command of state resources.[1] Yet the damage he had done to Britain's war machine was undeniable.

And the destruction he *almost* wreaked? Incalculable.

The year 1780 was the fifth year of a bloody civil war within the British Empire. Begun as a struggle for colonial self-government, it had grown into another global conflict over who would dominate a world of commerce, conquest, and enslavement. Patriots were smarting from the loss of Charleston and an army of 5,000 sorely needed men. But they had sources of hope, and among them was the story of the man called John the Painter (real name, James Aitken) and his extraordinary acts of sabotage. Britain's war effort depended, without question, on its strength at sea. If someone like Aitken could send a royal dockyard up in flames, then there must always be a chance that ordinary men and women could defeat the most powerful ruling class the world had ever seen. That was why Aitken was worth remembering.

---

1 *Pennsylvania Packet*, 25 July 1780.

In the early 1760s, when the crisis that led to the American Revolution was just getting started, Britain claimed an empire that stretched from the Ganges delta in Bengal to the swamps and forests of West Florida, including dozens of Caribbean islands, several West African coastal forts, and mainland North America's Atlantic shores. Trade was at the heart of this empire, both why it was built in the first place and how it was paid for. Tea and silk from distant China, cotton from India, sugar from Barbados and Jamaica, rice from South Carolina and tobacco from Virginia, and fish from the coastal banks of New England and Nova Scotia, all this and much more was carried every year across the oceans in a merchant fleet of thousands of ships to supply the wants of British consumers and contribute, in tax, the crucial revenue on which the British state was run.

Fixing our attention on commodities themselves, however, risks detracting from the hidden realm in which they were produced and moved around – the labour, with its sweat and strain, on which the commerce of the British Empire relied. That includes all the work, mostly done by women, which kept people going and raised children who became workers themselves. For the whole machine of Britain's power to survive, there needed to be millions of working men and women whose bodies provided the power and skill to make things people wanted, and to get them where they had to be. Aitken was one of them. He was a house painter, which meant that he mixed the ingredients of paints and then applied them to shopfronts and homes, sometimes to signs as well. In doing so, he made the world a slightly better place to look at.

Among these millions of workers in the British Empire, some 1.5 million were held in slavery at any given moment on the eve of the American Revolution. Two-thirds of these lived in the Caribbean, and most of the remaining third on the North American mainland, but there were thousands of enslaved people in Britain, too. Their enslavement was the most brutal and intense form of exploitative oppression that has ever been put into practice. It relied, in part, on wielding racecraft – the construction of a racial other through the use of markers like skin colour, building a deep prejudice into the ways most white people perceived those they defined as Black. The Atlantic slave trade, which transported millions of Africans to death or slavery, was an important component of Britain's empire in the eighteenth century.

That empire was also built on conquest and territorial expropriation. Since English settlers first arrived in North America in the 1600s, their use of the soil and its transformation into private property depended on another form of racialised prejudice, this time against Indigenous people. Settlers quickly came to feel that Native American claims to control and protect the land, no matter how many times they were affirmed by treaty, never ultimately trumped their own desire to occupy and use it. What was more, these two systems of racial thinking worked together – for slavery on such a scale could only be set up in far-off colonies, where labour was scarce and enslavers could dominate without resistance from a broader working population. Enslavement of Indigenous people only deepened the entanglement of slavery and conquest as the continent was remade for the benefit of Europeans.

Resistance to oppression and exploitation, whether on the scale of individuals or empires, is the historical force that animates the story in this book. When Aitken met an agent of the American Revolution in Paris in 1776, he was anxious to confirm that both men shared the same ideas about freedom. The agent reassured Aitken by telling him a version of an English proverb from two centuries before – the first great age of enclosure and capital. It had appeared in one of William Shakespeare's plays like this:

The smallest worm will turn being trodden on,
And doves will peck in safeguard of their brood.[2]

In other words, the agent explained to Aitken, it was simply a natural law that living things would stand up to abuse and tyranny. Futile or not, resistance was inevitable. Even the weakest creature prized its liberty.

Things are very often more complicated than that. People are complicit, in big ways and small, in the structures of their own oppression. Even the worm and the dove may sometimes punch down as well as up.

2 William Shakespeare, *Henry VI, Part 2* (Act 2, Scene 2).

But those complexities do not dissolve the basic insight that we share an urge for freedom. The Black poet Phillis Wheatley once wrote something similar. All people have that urge in them, she thought – 'It is impatient of oppression, and pants for deliverance.'[3] Richard Price, the Welsh philosopher whose work on civil liberty plays an important role in this book's story, thought the same. No word 'in the whole compass of language', he wrote, 'expresses so much of what is important and excellent' as the word *liberty*.[4]

The hypothesis of this book is that working people's everyday experience of oppression and exploitation, along with their shared urge to resist it and to work towards that thing called liberty, was a real, active force in shaping the world's history during the age of revolutions – and, indeed, in every other age. Even when they did not identify themselves as members of 'the working class' (a phrase that did not become popular until the nineteenth century), workers in Aitken's eighteenth century knew that they made up a majority of human beings. There were also, they often observed, a few who did not seem to work themselves but rather lived off others' work and held the whip hand over them – at times quite literally. In this book, which focuses on Britain and its colonies in mainland North America, I label the many 'the Atlantic working class'.[5]

---

3 Phillis Wheatley to Samson Occum, printed in *Connecticut Gazette*, 11 March 1774; quoted in David Waldstreicher, 'Ancients, Moderns, and Africans: Phillis Wheatley and the Politics of Empire and Slavery in the American Revolution', *Journal of the Early Republic* 37, no. 4 (Winter 2017), pp. 701–33.

4 Richard Price, *Observations on the Nature of Civil Liberty* (London, 1776), p. 5.

5 Many historians reject the use of class as a frame of analysis for places and periods where historical actors themselves did not use the term; in other words, where class-consciousness was not developed. This attitude has its roots in Edward Thompson's approach – he invoked an eighteenth-century world of 'class struggle without class' in Thompson, 'Eighteenth-Century English Society: Class Struggle Without Class?', *Social History* 3, no. 2 (May 1978), pp. 133–65 – and also in the cultural and linguistic turns of the late twentieth century. I believe that more is lost than gained by a rigid adherence to the rule of actors' categories, and that class as an objective relation is discernible through most of human history. See Keith Wrightson, 'Class', in David Armitage and Michael Braddick, eds, *The British Atlantic World, 1500–1800*, 2nd ed. (Palgrave Macmillan, 2009 [2002]), pp. 152–72; Simon Middleton and Billy G. Smith, 'Class and Early America: An Introduction', *William and Mary*

Notions of liberty were by no means exclusive to that working class, though. In fact, British ideas about freedom developed just as much from conflicts among noblemen and their associates as from the struggles of the poor. By the early eighteenth century, British culture at all levels possessed a well-developed tradition of appeals to freedom as the central principle of political life. The British Empire, as the historian of ideas David Armitage has written, was supposed to be 'Protestant, commercial, maritime, and free'.[6] While there were some who called for a community of property during the seventeenth-century English Revolution, its more enduring thinkers – men such as Algernon Sydney and Thomas Harrington – tended to have rather aristocratic views of just what made a person free and independent. It was these views that later caught on among wealthy American colonists, too.

As a result, the contradiction between workers' material contribution and their social subordination was matched by a further contradiction in the world of ideas. Britain's was an empire of freedom built on slavery and exploitation. Edmund Morgan, another historian, once wrote that the rise of liberty alongside slavery in North America – especially the richest colony, Virginia – was 'the central paradox of American history'.[7] Yet such a paradox also belonged to Britain. While the organs of the British state proclaimed the doctrine of freedom throughout the land during the eighteenth century, neither those who were kept in slavery nor those who lacked the property to qualify as independent quite knew how that applied to them. Some intellectuals expressed the cognitive dissonance of empire in clever satires and novels. Others, as the century

---

Quarterly 63, no. 2 (April 2006), pp. 211–20; Simon Middleton and Billy G. Smith, *Class Matters: Early North America and the Atlantic World* (University of Pennsylvania Press, 2010). On the twentieth-century politics of class analysis in early modern history, see Andy Wood, *The Politics of Social Conflict: The Peak Country, 1520–1770* (Cambridge University Press, 1999), pp. 1–26.

6 David Armitage, *The Ideological Origins of the British Empire* (Cambridge University Press, 2000), p. 195.

7 Edmund Morgan, 'American Slavery, American Freedom: The American Paradox', *Journal of American History* 59, no. 1 (July 1972), p. 6; see Morgan, *American Slavery, American Freedom: The Ordeal of Colonial Virginia* (W.W. Norton & Co., 1975).

went on, wrote increasingly clearly about how the people might secure real liberty.

I wrote this book because I think those ideas mattered, and not just for a small group of highly educated men. In almost all the other writing I have seen about James Aitken, going back to the 1930s ad man and naval historian William Bell Clark, there is always a turn away from showing him as a thinking person in his own right – a political actor, whose deeds were shaped by moral and intellectual assessments of the world around him. Historians seem to prefer to trace the root of Aitken's acts of sabotage to some hidden psychological defect – the cry for attention of a half-formed, childlike figure.[8] It is true, as you will see, that Aitken was no moral paragon. Far from it. But in this book, I treat him as someone who (in the words of the historian Jesse Lemisch) 'had a mind of his own and genuine reasons to act'.[9]

It is not that historians have ignored the problem of Britain's liberty paradox. Catherine Macaulay, one of the great critics of British pretentions to a state of freedom, was herself a historian of the seventeenth-century revolutions. More recently, in 1949, the Cambridge scholar Herbert Butterfield acknowledged that in 1780 Britain's ruling class faced something like a 'revolutionary moment' – their counterpart

---

8 William Bell Clark, 'John the Painter', *Pennsylvania Magazine of History and Biography* 63, no. 1 (January 1939), pp. 1–23; Jessica Warner, *John the Painter: The First Modern Terrorist* (Profile, 2004); Matthew Lockwood, *To Begin the World Over Again: How the American Revolution Devastated the Globe* (Yale University Press, 2019), pp. 46–60. In spite of its misleading subtitle, Jessica Warner's biography of James Aitken is a thoughtful and valuable piece of research, on which I have relied extensively. Warner's book remains the most thorough and detailed account of Aitken's life, and of the investigations that led to his capture and trial. This book does not substantially demur on points of fact regarding Aitken. It differs a great deal, however, in matters of perspective, context, and interpretation. This book's contribution lies in situating Aitken's actions in a very different story of the American Revolution, and of the Atlantic working class, than the one told by Warner or the other scholars cited in this note.

9 Jesse Lemisch, 'Jack Tar in the Streets: Merchant Seamen in the Politics of Revolutionary America', *William and Mary Quarterly* 25, no. 3 (July 1968), p. 401.

to France's storming of the Bastille nine years later.[10] A rich and important line of scholarship, from Caroline Robbins to Linda Colley and Kathleen Wilson, has investigated the ways empire, commerce, and conquest shaped British conceptions of freedom in the eighteenth century. Historians in the 1960s and 1970s looked to the 'radical' politics of two centuries earlier for clues about the possibilities of their own time.[11]

Relatively few, though, have tried to put the working-class fight for freedom at the centre of their stories. Most books about the American Revolution are stories of national becoming – although a growing number are about the boundaries of exclusion from that nation, and the struggles of the people it excluded. The story in this book is not about the birth of a nation or the founding of the United States. It is about a revolution that threatened to transform the Atlantic world by bringing down the British Empire. What might rise in that empire's place, on each side of the ocean, was an open question. Such uncertainties are natural in revolutions. They are what happen when ten thousand doves, a million worms begin to turn against their rulers and the rules that crush them down.

If this book aims to carry on the lineage of any other, it is Peter Linebaugh and Marcus Rediker's *The Many-Headed Hydra*. Published at the turn of the millennium, that book took the history-from-below that had been pioneered a generation earlier and applied it to the sweeping

10 Herbert Butterfield, *George III, Lord North, and the People* (G. Bell & Sons, 1949), p. vi.

11 Caroline Robbins, *The Eighteenth-Century Commonwealthman: Studies in the Transmission, Development and Circumstances of English Liberal Thought from the Restoration of Charles II Until the War with the Thirteen Colonies* (Harvard University Press, 1959); Linda Colley, *Britons: Forging the Nation, 1707–1837* (Yale University Press, 1992); Kathleen Wilson, *The Sense of the People: Politics, Culture and Imperialism in England, 1715–1785* (Cambridge University Press, 1995). For early histories of radicalism, see George Rudé, *Wilkes and Liberty: A Social Study of 1763–1774* (Oxford University Press, 1962); Carl Cone, *The English Jacobins: Reformers in Late 18th Century England* (Charles Scribner's Sons, 1968); Colin Bonwick, *English Radicals and the American Revolution* (University of North Carolina Press, 1977); Robert Toohey, *Liberty and Empire: British Radical Solutions to the American Problem, 1774–1776* (University Press of Kentucky, 1978); Linda Colley, 'Eighteenth-Century English Radicalism Before Wilkes', *Transactions of the Royal Historical Society* 31 (1981), pp. 1–19.

canvas of a British Atlantic spanning two centuries. It told stories of the motley crews of racially diverse sailors and dockside workers, not to mention pirates, rebel slaves, and revolutionaries, who fought for a common interest in the possibility of liberty – and how the modern state, emerging in this same moment, was formed in struggle with that common enterprise.[12] *Empire Ablaze* is a smaller book, with less epic ambitions. It is a reminder that the American Revolution took place in the midst of that great struggle, came from it, and helped shape it – one reason all of us should care about the revolution, on whichever side of the Atlantic we might live.

I have split the book into two parts, with the dividing line occurring roughly at the outbreak of armed conflict in the year 1775. The first half follows Aitken on a sort of tour of the Atlantic British Empire, in the decades leading up to the American Revolution. Sometimes leaving Aitken himself in the background, it provides an introduction to the working of the empire, as well as the forces that were tearing it asunder. Aitken's path took him from Edinburgh, where he was born, down to the empire's metropolis in London in a year of economic panic – 1772. From there, he crossed the Atlantic to Virginia and then travelled north to Philadelphia and other places in the colonies, returning to England in the early months of 1775. My telling begins with Virginia, so as to highlight from the start the fractured structure of an empire in crisis.

In the second half, I offer my account of Aitken's sabotage campaign – his plan to destroy the Royal Navy's crucial dockyards, to burn down

---

12 Peter Linebaugh and Marcus Rediker, *The Many-Headed Hydra: Sailors, Slaves, Commoners and the Hidden History of the Revolutionary Atlantic* (Verso, 2000). For an example of the original history-from-below, see Jesse Lemisch, 'The American Revolution Seen from the Bottom Up', in Barton J. Bernstein, ed., *Towards a New Past: Dissenting Essays in American History* (Pantheon Books, 1968), pp. 3–45. See also Marcus Rediker, 'A Motley Crew of Rebels: Sailors, Slaves, and the Coming of the American Revolution', in Ronald Hoffman and Peter Albert, eds, *The Transforming Hand of Revolution: Reconsidering the American Revolution as a Social Movement* (University Press of Virginia, 1996), pp. 155–98; Peter Linebaugh, *Red Round Globe Hot Burning: A Tale at the Crossroads of Commons and Closure, of Love and Terror, of Race and Class, and of Kate and Ned Despard* (University of California Press, 2021).

the second city of the British slave trade, and to ruin Britain's chances of defeating the American rebellion. But, before the action, we begin with words. Aitken was a British revolutionary inspired by arguments about freedom, and during the revolution there was no shortage of freedom talk in Britain. It was from the late autumn of 1776 until his execution in March 1777 that the most dramatic weeks of Aitken's life unfolded. I describe his deeds, his successes and failures, then his capture, his betrayal, and his death. In the last chapter, I give an account of the remainder of the war, and the unfinished struggle for a different kind of freedom among the Atlantic working class.

This is a short book because I would like you to read it, and there are far, far too many other things worth reading too. What that means is that not every detail or event, nor every layer of important context, is included here. Everything that is here should be understood in two ways – as part of an explanation of James Aitken's war against the British Empire, on the one hand, and, on the other, as part of an intellectual scaffolding that aims to link the story of the American Revolution to the wider, more important, and far longer story of the workers' quest for liberty. This is a story that belongs to everyone, one that deserves to be remembered.

In 1780, the memory of John the Painter gave courage to revolutionaries – reminding them that even a poor man, even the weakest among us, might have it within him to lay low the high and mighty. We today have no less need of such courage. We will continue to need it until the last empire has fallen.

PART I

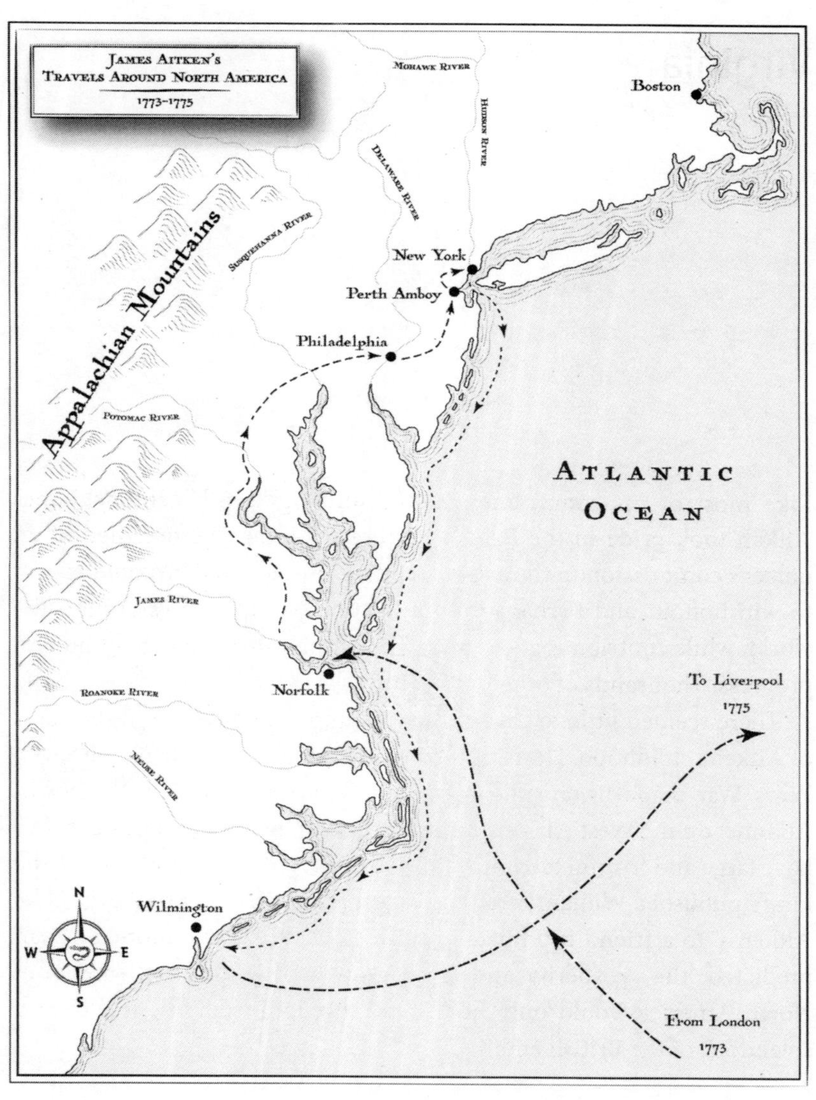

James Aitken's
Travels Around North America
1773–1775
Mohawk River
Hudson River
Delaware River
Boston
Susquehanna River
Appalachian Mountains
New York
Perth Amboy
Philadelphia
Potomac River
Atlantic Ocean
James River
Roanoke River
Norfolk
To Liverpool
1775
Neuse River
N
W E
S
Wilmington
From London
1773

1

Virginia

Like most of his countrymen in the mid-eighteenth century, James Aitken took pride in the British Empire. As a boy, he dreamed of an officer's commission in the army. Donning the red coat, he could expect to win honour and perhaps even a fortune on adventures around the world, while contributing – as he saw it – to the advancement of human progress. Thousands of other young men shared his hopes.

There seemed little to thwart Britain's imperial ambition in the years of Aitken's childhood. Decisive victories against France during the Seven Years War made Britain the dominant European power in the North Atlantic, on the West African coast, and in the Indian subcontinent. 'We have large and fruitful territories in every quarter of the globe', wrote the king's publisher William Strahan – born and raised in Edinburgh, like Aitken – to a friend in Philadelphia in 1772. What was more, Strahan predicted, the prosperity and rapid growth of British settlements in North America would only 'add to the strength, stability, wealth and splendour of the British empire'.[1]

---

1 William Strahan to David Hall, 2 December 1772, quoted in Peter Marshall, 'The British Empire and the American Revolution', *Huntington Library Quarterly* 27, no. 2 (February 1964), pp. 142–3.

Virginia, where Aitken arrived in 1773, was among the most 'fruitful' colonies in British North America. Along the rivers that fed into the Chesapeake Bay, huge estates spread across the once-fertile tidewater country, producing great quantities of tobacco for the British and colonial market. While very few held noble titles, Virginia's planter elite carried itself like an aristocracy, with the grand houses and expensive consumption habits to match. Ships sailing from British ports such as London and Glasgow could moor at the riverside wharves of the great estates and unload crates of mahogany chairs, silk waistcoats, and other manufactured goods, before filling their holds with hogsheads of tobacco for the return voyage. Virginia's staple economy did more than just support a few rich families. It also made a fine living for British merchants and manufacturers.[2]

The burden of this economic productivity, of course, fell squarely on the colony's enslaved workers. Virginia was the epicentre of racial slavery on the North American mainland, having pioneered the practices that defined the institution in the seventeenth century – including the law of *partus sequitur ventrem*, by which any child born to an enslaved mother was also condemned to slavery for life. Knowingly or not, the children of many white Virginian men were raised as the property of their father or one of his relatives. Slaveholding was an economic strategy, developed to address what was from the planters' perspective a shortage of cheap labour in a land-rich country. It was also, though, a sign of status and a marker of cultural identity. Other than land, it was in their slaves that

---

2 On the material culture of Britain's eighteenth-century empire, see Timothy Breen, *The Marketplace of Revolution: How Consumer Politics Shaped American Independence* (Oxford University Press, 2005); Steven Bullock, *Tea Sets and Tyranny: The Politics of Politeness in Early America* (University of Pennsylvania Press, 2017); Zara Anishanslin, *Portrait of a Woman in Silk: Hidden Histories of the British Atlantic World* (Yale University Press, 2018); and for the wider Atlantic, Ashli White, *Revolutionary Things: Material Culture and Politics in the Late Eighteenth-Century Atlantic World* (Yale University Press, 2023). On Virginia's tobacco economy, see Timothy Breen, *Tobacco Culture: The Mentality of the Great Tidewater Planters on the Eve of Revolution* (Princeton University Press, 1985); Allan Kulikoff, *Tobacco and Slaves: The Development of Southern Cultures in the Chesapeake, 1680–1800* (University of North Carolina Press, 1986).

nearly all the planters' wealth lay. Virginia's prosperity, and its social order, depended on its Black population.

In the tidewater counties adjacent to the Chesapeake Bay, Virginia's most prominent families lived among the people they enslaved, juxtaposing the extremes of the colonial hierarchy. By the 1770s, the Piedmont region further west was also home to large plantations, such as Thomas Jefferson's Monticello. Deeper inland, though, away from easy access to the rivers and Atlantic trade, a different kind of settlement pattern prevailed. In this backcountry, Virginia was a frontier of small farmers, far removed from the great tidewater plantations. While many settlers owned some slaves, there were others who eschewed the practice. Religious dissenters expressed a form of opposition to the colony's Anglican elite, while conflicts frequently flared up between tenants or squatters and land speculators from the east. Wealth and geography, as well as race, created lines of tension in Virginia society.

Those tensions had only intensified since the British victory in the Seven Years War. Months after the treaty with France was signed in 1763, an alliance of Indigenous forces in the contested region around the Great Lakes launched a series of attacks on British forts. They were fighting to protect the territory west of the Appalachian Mountains – land secured by treaty after treaty, but which many colonists now saw as a target for settlement and speculation. British authorities hoped to prevent further conflict with Indigenous nations by outlawing white land claims beyond the so-called Proclamation Line. Their efforts were met with contempt by would-be settlers. For much of the following decade, those settlers mixed violence against local Indigenous people with bitter condemnation of the eastern elites they deemed complicit in restricting their access to land.[3]

Meanwhile, migrants from Europe continued to flow into the Appalachian frontier zone. Many came from the disunited German

---

3 On the eighteenth century's Appalachian borderland, see Eric Hinderaker, *Elusive Empires: Constructing Colonialism in the Ohio Valley, 1673–1800* (Cambridge University Press, 1997); Patrick Griffin, *American Leviathan: Empire, Nation, and Revolutionary Frontier* (Hill and Wang, 2007); François Furstenberg, 'The Significance of the Trans-Appalachian Frontier in Atlantic History', *American Historical Review* 113, no. 3 (June 2008), pp. 647–77.

states, bringing their language deep into the American interior. Larger numbers travelled from the Irish and Scottish countryside – whole families, even whole communities, moving west in search of land and opportunity for themselves and their descendants. Almost all were Protestants, however varied their specific sects. Ignoring the powerful Indigenous presence that so worried British authorities, they tended to see Britain's victory against the Catholic French as a sign of providential destiny in the New World. Not that they were partisans of British power. It was often those least satisfied with the conditions of their old lives who sought new ones across the Atlantic, provided they could muster the resources for the journey. Such folk tended to put little trust in government to help them out.

It was one thing for a man like William Strahan to look at the empire in 1772 and see increasing 'strength, stability, wealth and splendour'. Plenty of others, including his friend Benjamin Franklin, perceived the growing – and explosive – set of contradictions that ran through it all.

The project of empire involved more than just conquest and occupation, redrawing the lines on maps. The real challenge lay in harnessing the motion of people, goods, and money from one place to another. Military strength depended on revenue, which depended on trade, which, in turn, depended on the population of producers and consumers in the right places and with access to the right resources. Sometimes, it seemed to run almost like clockwork. But not always. In fact, when James Aitken arrived in Virginia in 1773, things were already beginning to unravel.

To understand the world in which James Aitken now arrived, we could start eight years earlier and nearly 10,000 miles away, in India. That was when Mughal emperor Alam II signed a treaty giving the British East India Company tax-gathering powers in Bengal and two neighbouring provinces. Alam's concession was another outcome of Britain's success against the French and their allies in the Seven Years War. The Company's rapacious use of its new powers would have dire consequences for the people of Bengal. It was also one spark in the sequence of incendiary events that tore apart the British Empire in North America.

By 1769, the impact of the Company's extractive regime could be felt all over Bengal. When draught was added to the mix that year, the resulting famine killed as many as 3 million people, devastating the region – and, of course, its economy. Inevitably, the destruction cut into the Company's own revenue, forcing it into financial difficulties as it struggled to keep up with payments in both India and England. Company stock became highly volatile, as traders in London and Amsterdam tried to speculate on its future. There were some powerful men, including Company directors, whose fortunes depended on the stock price holding firm. Others, such as the Aberdeen-born banker James Fordyce, bet heavily on a continued fall. In the spring of 1772, Fordyce's gamble failed spectacularly. His firm's collapse triggered the worst financial crisis since the fabled South Sea Bubble.

British imperial power and economic development had been rooted in financialisation since the seventeenth century, but the trend only accelerated in the decade after 1763. In that time, dozens of new banks grew up, offering finance for projects aimed at capitalising on Britain's apparent triumph – new plantations in the Caribbean, for example, and luxury housing developments in the imperial cities of London and Edinburgh. Cheap credit had made such investments possible. But when the panic started and bills suddenly came due, the web of debt that spanned the empire became an ever-tightening noose. Wages were stopped, contracts breached, and 'many families reduced to want and beggary', as one Virginian in London put it.[4]

In Virginia itself, the recession hit hard – all the worse because it shattered a period of relative prosperity, and therefore higher spending on credit. The consequences of financial crisis 'have extended to this part of the world to a violent degree', one colonist warned his correspondent in Liverpool. Unless the tobacco price rebounded, he went on, 'I don't see how we shall be enabled to discharge our debts on your side of the water.'[5] Debt-loaded Virginia planters faced ruin, and from their

---

4 Robert Orme to William Ridge, 1 July 1772, quoted in Nick Bunker, *An Empire on the Edge: How Britain Came to Fight America* (Alfred A. Knopf, 2014), pp. 82–3.

5 William Allason to John Backhouse, 15 July 1773, quoted in Richard Sheridan, 'The British Credit Crisis of 1772 and the American Colonies', *Journal of Economic History* 20, no. 2 (June 1960), p. 175.

perspective it came at the hands of the unbalanced, unstable imperial economy.

Virginia's planter elite had been trying for years to scale back the colony's reliance on imports. In 1767, when the government in London introduced a series of new taxes on commodities like glass, paper, and tea, colonists rallied behind boycott measures aimed at both punishing British merchants and teaching consumers to do without. George Washington, one of Virginia's most substantial landowners, was one of the non-importation movement's backers. He had no intention of giving up the luxuries and status symbols that helped to define him as a gentleman of substance. But, like many planters, he did hope to break the economic hold of British creditors.

This struggle for economic disentanglement was particularly fraught when it came to one imported commodity Virginians had long relied upon – enslaved people. While colonists protested against taxes imposed by Parliament in the late 1760s, Virginia's assembly was trying to ramp up the duties charged on captives brought into the colony. Doing so, the legislators hoped, would help prevent cash leaving the Virginia economy and stop planters from getting deeper into debt. It would support the growth of a domestic slave trade, making American colonists less dependent on African and Caribbean imports. It might even boost tobacco prices by cutting the growth of new plantations.[6]

In April 1772, right around the time that James Fordyce's gamble on East India Company stock was falling apart, the Virginia assembly took its campaign to curb slave imports a step further. Its members signed a unanimous address to the king in England, asking him to let the colonists shut down the transatlantic slave trade altogether. They even had the gall to claim humanitarian motives.

'The importation of slaves into the colonies from the coast of Africa hath long been considered as a trade of great inhumanity', wrote the

---

6 For the politics of slavery and settler colonialism in Virginia on the eve of revolution, see Woody Holton, *Forced Founders: Indians, Debtors, and Slaves in the Making of the American Revolution in Virginia* (University of North Carolina Press, 1999).

Virginia legislators – almost all of them slave owners themselves.[7] They did not expect that kind of argument to sway the British government, though. Far more important was their premonition that the slave trade, and the predominance of slavery itself, might soon 'endanger the very existence' of Britain's American colonies. Virginia's planter elite had come to see dependence on slavery as an economic problem, reducing innovation and stifling growth. They were also terrified of the kind of uprisings that had rocked Jamaica through the 1760s. Besides, the well-established planters already had all the enslaved labour they needed. Cutting off the flow of imports might hit their western competitors, but it would do no harm to their own bottom lines.

From London, of course, things looked different. The Atlantic slave trade had been crucial to the growth of Britain's Caribbean and American possessions through the eighteenth century. Even in New England, where there were relatively few enslaved workers, a great deal of profit depended on the shipping and supply needs of plantation economies further south. Merchants in British port cities were likewise committed to the slave trade and the cash crops that went with it.[8] When Virginians asked for the right to throw a wrench into the gears of the whole system, the answer was a resounding no.

Then the recession hit. Banks collapsed, tobacco prices dipped, and creditors called in their debts. It was not only the rebuffed Virginia assemblymen who were angry and frustrated in 1773. That July, one county courthouse was burned to the ground. Debtors fought with

---

7 Virginia Colony to George III, 1 April 1772; Thomas Jefferson Papers at the Library of Congress.

8 On the working of the Atlantic economy and the centrality of slavery, see John McCusker and Russell Menard, *The Economy of British America, 1607–1789* (University of North Carolina Press, 1991); Kenneth Morgan, *Slavery, Atlantic Trade and the British Economy, 1660–1800* (Cambridge University Press, 2001); Cathy Matson, ed., *The Economy of Early America: Historical Perspectives and New Directions* (Penn State University Press, 2006). Beginning with Eric Williams, *Capitalism and Slavery* (University of North Carolina Press, 1944), there has been extensive scholarly debate surrounding the impact of slavery on economic development in Britain, but for a recent and powerful intervention, see Maxine Berg and Pat Hudson, *Slavery, Capitalism and the Industrial Revolution* (Polity Press, 2023).

sheriffs over seizures of their property, and some storekeepers took to carrying pistols for their own protection. Boycotts were no longer necessary as importers reduced their orders. Planters began to fear the rising social tension. Conditions were a long way, yet, from revolutionary. They were, however, poor advertisements for the empire's 'strength, stability . . . and splendour'.

Just as settler conquest was the basis of land ownership, racial slavery was at the heart of eighteenth-century Virginia's economy and social hierarchy. Whatever the planter elite said about stopping the transatlantic slave trade, none was prepared to sacrifice their own interests to bring an end to slavery itself. It was people of African and sometimes Indigenous descent, bound for life and often subjected to brutal, dehumanising treatment, who did the vast bulk of the colony's work. Yet there were other forms of unfree labour in Virginia, too. Not every European arriving in the New World encountered it as a land of liberty.[9]

Some of those new migrants, for example, were convicted criminals. The sentence of 'transportation' to the American colonies had been used for most of the eighteenth century as an alternative to the death penalty for crimes such as assault and theft. It was also applied regularly to those whose crimes were more vaguely defined: rogues and vagabonds who presented a threat to social order, and a potential burden to the communities they entered. For a few British merchants, the trade in convicts offered a steady rate of profit. Hundreds were shipped out each year, mostly to Virginia and its Chesapeake neighbours, where they would be sold for a term of labour as a servant.

One such unwilling transatlantic migrant, whose legend began to circulate in 1773, was a young woman named Sarah Wilson. Brought to Maryland two years before, she had escaped her master and travelled

---

9 The broad history of Atlantic labour regimes is analysed in Christopher Tomlins, *Freedom Bound: Law, Labor, and Civic Identity in Colonizing English America, 1580–1865* (Cambridge University Press, 2010); and for the spectrum of unfreedom in early American labour, see Seth Rockman, 'The Unfree Origins of American Capitalism', in Matson, ed., *Economy of Early America*, pp. 335–61.

south, adopting the identity of Princess Susanna Carolina Matilda, sister – so she claimed – of Queen Charlotte herself. According to accounts first published in a New York paper, Wilson carried off the ruse so well that she exacted 'heavy contributions' from a succession of southern gentlemen seeking the 'honour to kiss her hand'.[10] Even in the 1770s, and especially in places like South Carolina, wealthy Americans were by no means immune to the charms and promises of supposed royalty.

Wilson's alleged exploits indicate one reason servants might have found it easier to escape from their bondage than most enslaved people of African descent – they could pass easily in white society. Nor was escape the only route to freedom that a transportee could hope for. Once their term of service was completed, they could strike out on their own behalf like any other European immigrant.

A mythology quickly arose about the former criminals who managed to transform themselves into respectable, property-owning colonists. In Virginia, 'many a Newgate bird becomes a great man', as Moll Flanders's mother put it in Daniel Defoe's novel. Of course, the stories were often too good to be true, even when they claimed to be non-fiction. Joshua Dudley, for example, was transported in 1772. Two years later, he reported his adventures to a London paper. 'I lived in the most delightful manner', he wrote, instantly winning the trust of his wealthy, widowed mistress. Naturally, her timely death made Dudley master of her plantation and slaves. It also left him in the welcome company of her eighteen-year-old daughter, Isabella.[11]

British readers might believe such providential wonders, but the *Virginia Gazette* warned that the whole thing was 'a most notorious falsity'. Dudley, in fact, was still in service to the men who had first bought his contract.[12] It was not the first time he had been caught lying, either. His transportation was the penalty for perjury, after he claimed to

10 *Rivington's New York Gazetteer*, 13 May 1773, quoted in Gwenda Morgan and Peter Rushton, *Eighteenth-Century Criminal Transportation: The Formation of the Criminal Atlantic* (Palgrave Macmillan, 2004), pp. 85–6.

11 *Morning Chronicle and London Advertiser*, 18 October 1774.

12 *Virginia Gazette* (Purdie), 10 March 1775, quoted in Peter Rushton and Gwenda Morgan, *Treason and Rebellion in the British Atlantic, 1685–1800: Legal Responses to Threatening the State* (Bloomsbury, 2020), p. 136.

know the details of an elaborate Catholic plot to set fire to the Portsmouth royal dockyard. The fire, in 1770, was real, and Dudley sought the £1,000 reward for information on it. His tale of a plot, though, like his consummate good fortune in Virginia, was pure fabrication.

Notwithstanding the more wide-eyed fantasies, the possibility of securing a better life in the New World did lure migrants across the Atlantic through the eighteenth century. For those without the money to pay their own way, one solution was indentured servitude. Men and women who took such terms would be contracted for as little as four years of labour – considerably less than a transported convict. They might also agree in advance what kind of labour they were undertaking. Others, less skilled or perhaps more desperate, might agree a term of service with a ship's captain to be auctioned off at his destination. Either path came with all the uncertainty of migration across the ocean.[13]

John Harrower, a small-time merchant whose credit had run dry, left his home in the Shetland Islands in late 1773. He came to London 'friendless', seeking business or work anywhere, until 'being reduced to the last shilling . . . [he] was obliged to go to Virginia for four years as a schoolmaster'. Apart from his bed and board, Harrower was promised £5 pay for the entire four years' service.[14] His experience was hardly unusual, especially in years of economic hardship. More than half the servants who shipped out from London had already come there from somewhere else in search of work.

One of these migrants was twenty-year-old James Aitken, arrived from Edinburgh in 1772. Aitken did not come with the same skills or genteel appearance as Harrower, who owned more than one coat and

---

13 On migration to the eighteenth-century colonies in general, see Bernard Bailyn, *Voyagers to the West: A Passage in the Peopling of America on the Eve of the Revolution* (Knopf, 1986); Ned Landsman, 'Migration and Settlement', in Daniel Vickers, ed., *A Companion to Colonial America* (Blackwell, 2006), pp. 76–98. For one case from slightly earlier in the century, see Susan Klepp and Billy G. Smith, eds, *The Infortunate: The Voyage and Adventures of William Moraley, an Indentured Servant* (Penn State University Press, 1992).

14 'Diary of John Harrower, 1773–1776', *American Historical Review* 6, no. 1 (October 1900), pp. 70, 72.

ruffled shirt as well as possessing a fine hand for writing. Rather than a number of years' service, Aitken's indenture was set to the value of £24 Virginia money – the equivalent of £18 sterling. When he reached the colony, the captain who had taken him on board sold Aitken's contract to a local man.[15] He would be free once he worked off the contract's value. But, without a fixed term of years, there was bound to be a struggle over just how much work Aitken owed to his new master. It was an unenviable situation.

For Aitken, the main purpose of his journey had been to escape from London and its close surroundings. He was running from some bad choices. As they had done for so many young migrants before him, the colonies offered something of a blank slate, another chance at life. On the other hand, the price for his passage across the Atlantic was a heavy one. As a servant, he possessed his wits and the privilege of his white skin, but little else. With the colony's economy deep in recession, the young man's chances of landing on his feet seemed slim indeed.

Just as James Aitken was arriving in Virginia bound to servitude, rumours of freedom had begun to spread among the colony's enslaved people. Virginia's Black population, by the 1770s, was a well-established and highly networked community. Family ties and plenty of other relationships crossed the boundaries between plantations, and it was common for people to visit one another behind the backs of masters and overseers. It did not take long for news and new ideas to circulate, however much the enslavers relied on keeping their captives ignorant. In 1773, the word on everyone's lips was a name: Somerset.

James Somerset was not the name first given to the little boy born in West Africa around 1741. It was given to him eight years later, after he was trafficked into slavery in Virginia, by the man who bought him, the Scottish-born merchant Charles Stewart. For twenty years, Somerset lived and worked in slavery to Stewart, moving from Virginia to Massachusetts as his master's career prospered. In 1769, Stewart

---

15 [James Aitken,] *Life of James Aitken* (Winchester, 1777), pp. 17–18.

brought Somerset with him to England, and there two years later – after being baptised in a London church – the thirty-year-old slipped away and fled his life of slavery. Captured two months later by his owner's hired men, and threatened with sale off to a Jamaica plantation, Somerset became the centre of the century's most celebrated trial.

British authorities, including the chief justice Lord Mansfield, had in fact done all they could in the preceding years to keep the question of slavery out of the English courts. To have the question litigated would expose the contradiction between Britain's vaunted liberty and its entanglement with racial slavery. It was Stewart's stubbornness and the strength of his case that finally forced their hands, for nobody denied that Somerset indeed belonged to him under colonial law. With the support of a small English anti-slavery movement, Somerset won freedom from his captors. A servant could not be deported from England without his consent, ruled Mansfield, and thus he was ordered to be set loose from his chains.[16]

To observers like Benjamin Franklin, the limits of the ruling were clear. It had won the freedom of 'a *single slave*', while doing nothing to prevent the trade 'whereby so many *hundreds of thousands* are dragged into slavery'.[17] Yet abolitionists in London declared the case a triumph, insisting it meant freedom for any enslaved person who set foot on English soil. Transformed and inflated by both hopeful and anxious audiences, news of the Somerset decision was soon racing around the British Empire.

In eastern Virginia, where planter families often lived among enslaved majorities, anxiety about escapes and uprisings was already at a high pitch. Ever since 1760, when a major insurrection known as Tacky's Revolt rocked the island of Jamaica, the Virginia elite had begun to

---

16 On the Somerset case, its legal background, and its limitations, see George Van Cleve, 'Somerset's Case and Its Antecedents in Imperial Perspective', *Law and History Review* 24, no. 3 (Fall 2006), pp. 601–46, with responses by Daniel Hulsebosch, Ruth Paley, and Van Cleve in the same issue.

17 Benjamin Franklin, *London Chronicle*, 20 June 1772.

seriously worry about organised resistance to the slave regime.[18] Arthur Lee in the *Virginia Gazette* recalled that the freemen of ancient Rome were 'brought to the very brink of ruin by the insurrections of their slaves'.[19] Such fears were one motive behind their efforts to reduce or even abolish the transatlantic slave trade. Captives just arrived from Africa were, after all, among those most likely to rise against a system they had not been born into.

Escape, sometimes coinciding with the murder of planters and overseers, was widespread in the eighteenth-century Chesapeake. Advertising freedom seekers – escapees – and the rewards for their capture helped prop up colonial newspapers. Advertisers offered details of the fugitives' appearance and likely clothing to ensure they could not pass unnoticed on the road to freedom. Such adverts were part of the infrastructure of Virginia's racialised surveillance society. They also sometimes speculated on the likely movements and intentions of those who escaped, inadvertently recording a history of self-emancipation.[20]

In the wake of the Somerset decision, one Virginia enslaver advertised two runaways from his plantation. One was a woman in her late twenties named Amy, 'well made' and with a 'mild soft way of speaking'. The other, a nineteen-year-old called Bacchus, had been born in Africa. Their enslaver believed that both had tried to pass as free people, perhaps using false papers. Yet both now aimed 'to get out of the colony, particularly to Britain, where they imagine they will be free'. That reaching English soil would mean freedom was 'a notion now too

18 See Vincent Brown, *Tacky's Revolt: The Story of an Atlantic Slave War* (Harvard University Press, 2020); Trevor Burnard, *Jamaica in the Age of Revolution* (University of Pennsylvania Press, 2020).

19 Philanthropus [Arthur Lee], *Virginia Gazette*, 19 March 1767.

20 See Freedom on the Move, a database of these adverts based at Cornell University: freedomonthemove.org. For the role of such adverts in print culture, see David Waldstreicher, 'Reading the Runaways: Self-Fashioning, Print Culture, and Confidence in Slavery in the Eighteenth-Century Mid-Atlantic', *William and Mary Quarterly* 56, no. 2 (April 1999), pp. 243–72; and Waldstreicher, *Runaway America: Benjamin Franklin, Slavery, and the American Revolution* (Hill and Wang, 2004).

prevalent' among Virginia's enslaved people, wrote the advertiser – one that caused their masters great 'vexation'.[21]

Port towns such as Norfolk and Fredericksburg, some of Virginia's few urban centres, were the kind of places runaways like Amy and Bacchus hoped to reach in order to find passage on a ship out of the colony. It was also in such towns, where there was hope of work and some sort of community, that most of Virginia's free Black people lived. Planters often viewed cities with deep suspicion, in part because they brought together landless workers who threatened the social and racial order. It was not only slaves, after all, who sought to free themselves from lives of labour and oppression.

Sancho, an enslaved mixed-race carpenter, and Elizabeth Beaver, a 'white servant woman', escaped together in early 1774. Sancho was forty and carried a large knife. Elizabeth was twenty, had 'a fresh complexion', and had taken with her a good quilt and many other items from her master's house. 'I expect they will change their names, and endeavour to pass for husband and wife, as free people', their former master speculated in his advert for their capture.[22] Working together, the pair demonstrated the overlapping interests of bound labourers across Virginia's spectrum of unfreedom. In their solidarity, they posed an even greater threat to the stability of the planters' regime.

James Aitken, too, soon joined the list of escaped servants. 'It was never my intention to remain longer with the captain than suited my conveniency', he recalled later.[23] Having made it to America, he preferred a fugitive's life to one of indentured servitude. It would be no surprise if, like other escapees, Aitken stole clothing and valuables from his new master before absconding into the night. Unlike Amy, Bacchus, and the

---

21 *Virginia Gazette* (Purdie and Dixon), 30 September 1773. See Peter Wood, '"The Dream Deferred": Black Freedom Struggles on the Eve of White Independence', in Gary Okihiro, ed., *In Resistance: Studies in African, Caribbean, and Afro-American History* (University of Massachusetts Press, 1986), p. 169; and Gerald Mullin, *Flight and Rebellion: Slave Resistance in Eighteenth-Century Virginia* (Oxford University Press, 1972).

22 *Virginia Gazette* (Rind), 17 March 1774.

23 [Aitken,] *Life*, p. 18.

others who took inspiration from James Somerset, though, Aitken had no wish to set sail back to England. That was precisely where he was running from.

On top of the recession, and the deep vexation caused by news of the Somerset ruling, Virginia's planter elite was troubled in 1773 by serious concerns about the British government's plan for the empire. That year, for the first time, many of the colony's most powerful and well-respected gentlemen became convinced that there was a concerted effort underway to destroy the civil liberties of the American colonists. One might even call it a conspiracy – and it went to the very top.

What pushed Virginia's gentlemen to this conclusion was the government's response to an incident the year before, in the little northern colony of Rhode Island. The *Gaspee* was a Royal Navy schooner engaged in enforcing controversial customs regulations along the North American coast. According to Rhode Islanders, it had spent six months stopping local merchant vessels and seizing goods with marked enthusiasm, while showing disdain for the colony's government. Then, one night in June, while chasing a potential prize, the *Gaspee* ran hard aground not far from the town of Providence. Before the tide could lift the schooner free, a band of men rowed out from shore and fought their way on board. After evacuating the handcuffed crew, they set the ship ablaze.[24]

The destruction of the *Gaspee* was not the first time that Rhode Islanders had burned a Royal Navy customs vessel they accused of interfering with their trade. The same thing had happened to the *Liberty*, boarded in Newport harbour in 1769. Since then, however, the king had installed a more hard-line government. After the 1770 fire at Portsmouth, acts of arson targeting the navy were firmly on authorities' radar. So,

---

24 For a thorough account, see Peter Messer, 'A Most Insulting Violation: The Burning of the HMS *Gaspee* and the Delaying of the American Revolution', *New England Quarterly* 88, no. 4 (December 2015), pp. 582–622; see also Rushton and Morgan, *Treason and Rebellion*, pp. 140–3.

when news of the *Gaspee* reached London, it provoked a furious response. The attack, it was decided, amounted to high treason, and a high commission was established to investigate. Clearly, the colonists could not be trusted to address the situation responsibly. The culprits, once identified, were to be brought to England for their trial.

It was this insult to colonial legal institutions, and attack on the colonists' right to be tried by a jury of their peers rather than one 3,000 miles overseas, that got the attention of Virginia assemblymen. Writing from London, the Virginian Arthur Lee declared the commission an important milestone on the route to despotism. He implored his countrymen to 'stand forth in the glorious cause of freedom . . . to prevent the fastening of the infernal chains now forging for you'.[25] A few months later, the assembly declared that it was 'much disturbed by various rumours and reports of proceedings tending to deprive them of their ancient, legal, and constitutional rights'. They voted unanimously to start working directly with the other colonies, establishing a committee of correspondence.[26]

In the end, the high commission never managed to bring anyone to trial for the burning of the *Gaspee*. The men who organised and carried out the attack included some of Rhode Island's most influential citizens, after all. Few people were willing to give evidence against them, and those who did – like the dark-skinned, sixteen-year-old servant Aaron Briggs – were easily dismissed by prejudiced colonists. Yet the commission had certainly helped escalate the struggle between colonies and government in London, fuelling Americans' fears of a conspiracy against their liberty.

All that helped set the stage for the next bombshell to hit the colonies in 1773: the Tea Act. One of the original subjects of increased taxation in the 1760s, tea was an everyday consumer luxury in the colonies. Efforts to cut tea consumption during the earlier non-importation movements

---

25 Americanus [Arthur Lee], *Virginia Gazette* (Rind), 28 January 1773.

26 Virginia Resolutions Establishing a Committee of Correspondence, 12 March 1773; Avalon Project. For the Virginia response to the *Gaspee* incident, see Joseph DeVaro Jr, 'The Impact of the Gaspee Affair on the Coming of the Revolution, 1772–1773' (PhD diss., Case Western Reserve University, 1973), pp. 306–9.

met with little success, partly because a great deal of the tea drunk in the colonies was not actually taxed at all – it was so-called Dutch tea, smuggled from other European empires rather than imported from Britain as the law required. When the Tea Act granted the struggling East India Company permission to import directly to America, slashing the taxes owed on legal tea, it threatened to disrupt established patterns of illicit trade. In the context of the *Gaspee* fallout, it also appeared as another example of tightening imperial control.[27]

None of the four port cities due to receive the Company's tea was in Virginia – the nearest was Charleston, South Carolina. By the time the tea ships set sail for America that autumn, though, much of Virginia's elite was already committed to collective resistance against the 'infernal chains' that Arthur Lee had warned about. The intercolonial committee network Virginians initiated that spring was one step closer to the Continental Congress that would be established the following year. Meanwhile, James Aitken was on his way north towards the city of Philadelphia, where a consignment of East India Company tea was due to arrive that winter. What was he doing in America at all? For that story, we need to begin across the ocean in his hometown, Edinburgh.

27 For the Tea Act and surrounding politics, see Bunker, *Empire on the Edge*; and James Fichter, *Tea: Consumption, Politics, and Revolution, 1773–1776* (Cornell University Press, 2023).

2

Edinburgh

When the handsome young prince Charles Edward Stuart and his army of Jacobite rebels paraded through Edinburgh in September 1745, a crowd of thousands came to cheer for him. Yet, as one embittered rebel leader put it later, 'not one of the mob who were so fond of seeing him ever asked to enlist in his service'.[1] By the following spring, the rebellion lay crushed at the hands of British forces – hundreds dead on the battlefield at Culloden, and vicious reprisals ripping through the Scottish countryside. The outcome of the struggle was further entrenchment of the London-based Hanoverian supremacy. Scotland would henceforth be more integrated in the British imperial project, much to the economic benefit of the capitalist class.[2] For the ordinary people of Edinburgh, people like James Aitken's parents, the Jacobite uprising was no more than a fleeting spectacle. It had promised just as little as it ultimately delivered.

1 Lord Elcho, *A Short Account of the Affairs of Scotland in the Years 1744, 1745, and 1746*, ed. Sir Evan Charteris (Edinburgh, 1907), p. 261.

2 For the battle, see Murray Pittock, *Culloden: Great Battles* (Oxford University Press, 2016). On the transformation of Scotland in the eighteenth century, see T.M. Devine and J.R. Young, eds, *Eighteenth-Century Scotland: New Perspectives* (Tuckwell Press, 1999).

A generation later, during the American Revolution, there were two kinds of Scots the rebel colonists treated with deep suspicion. One was the highlander, who came to British North America in search of security and land. Some of these were exiles, pardoned for their participation in the uprising of '45. Others were simply fleeing the repression and economic change that spread across Highland communities in the decades that followed. These highlanders may have crossed the Atlantic, but they did not leave behind Scottish identity and culture – including the networks of loyalty and honour that had often enmeshed them in the Jacobite cause. On the frontiers of colonial settlement, they aimed to re-establish the kinds of community and independent rural life that were already being decimated back in Britain.

From the perspective of more established American colonists, especially the educated elite, these highlanders were primitive and backward-looking people. They may have been rebels, but in a deeper sense their politics were tainted by servility. Who, after all, would want to fight on behalf of the Stuart dynasty, a band of corrupt, syphilitic papists? By contrast, most Americans identified with the so-called Whig tradition, originating with those who, in 1688, had overthrown Charles Stuart's grandfather James and installed the Protestant regime of the Dutch stadtholder, William of Orange, and his wife Mary (Charles's aunt). They defined themselves in terms of progress and imperial expansion – the spread of commerce and the Protestant religion, and of a politics in which representation was taken seriously, at least for the propertied.

The other Scots considered with suspicion in the colonies were altogether different from the highlanders. These were the merchants and storekeepers who, by the 1770s, had established a formidable network of credit lines across the American countryside. That network generally led back to port cities such as Glasgow, hub of the transatlantic tobacco trade. As tobacco cultivation spread westwards in colonies like Virginia, it was very often Scots who linked these new producers to the wider market. When tobacco prices dipped or crops failed, planters took on debts that gradually left them beholden to the merchants – just as the grand tidewater planters were, on a much larger scale, to their London,

Bristol, or Liverpool agents. 'We all know that we are slaves to the power of the merchants', Virginians lamented in 1771.[3]

Scottish merchants' growing power in America, resented as it was by the colonists, was part of a larger story of economic development in the mid-eighteenth century. New trade links around the British Empire and more efficient, market-oriented agriculture were both driven by flows of financial investment, including new banking houses connected to networks of English capital. Rents were forced up, squeezing Highland communities that had not already been shattered by the fallout of rebellion. At the same time, the population in the fertile central lowlands and the thriving cities grew. Beneath the merchants, the expanding professional class, and a newly commercial gentry and nobility, Scotland's spectacular progress rested on the intensifying labour of tenant farmers, urban artisans, and propertyless workers.

In fact, Scotland's mid-century transformation was the very model of how some contemporaries came to think about human progress. Professors like Adam Smith and Adam Ferguson, who combined studies in moral philosophy with the newfangled science of political economy, came up with theories of development that made intensifying economic productivity and inequality seem like the outcome of a natural process – rather than expressions of power and ongoing struggle. Their Scottish Enlightenment thought was not uncritical of capitalism's effects. They perceived the damage it could do to both moral and physical health, on an individual and social level. But they were sure, nonetheless, that it represented progress. Those who sought to combat inequality were, like the Jacobites, simply resisting the inevitable.

Scotland's experience within the British Empire was different from that of the North American colonies – or of Ireland, come to that. In the first place, Scotland was an economically integrated part of the imperial core. The only restrictions on the trade of Scottish merchants were those that applied equally in London, Bristol, and Liverpool, and there were no

---

3 'To the Planters of Virginia', *Virginia Gazette* (Rind), 31 October 1771, quoted in J.H. Soltow, 'Scottish Traders in Virginia, 1750–1775', *Economic History Review* 12, no. 1 (1959), p. 83.

taxes for transporting goods across the English border. That integration was crucial to Scotland's rapid commercial development – and it was quite distinct from the regime of duties and restrictions that applied to the overseas colonies.

In the second place, Scotland after 1707 had no representative political institutions of its own. Unlike the colonies, Scots did not vote for an assembly to make their laws. Instead, they sent a few MPs to Westminster. Political culture in mid-eighteenth-century Scotland was, therefore, as underdeveloped as its economic progress was prodigious. For much of the country's elite, that was hardly a problem. Their interests aligned neatly with the empire to which they were subordinated. So long as English capital continued to flow through Scottish banks, and colonial tobacco through Scottish ports, the burden of government could be safely entrusted to the metropole. After the failure of '45, there were few left to challenge London's rule.

Prosperity in Edinburgh during the middle decades of the century meant population growth. People arrived to seek their fortune, and families had more children who lived. But, until the late 1760s, the boundaries of the city scarcely grew. Hemmed in by steep hills, medieval walls, and the man-made North Loch, Edinburgh's citizens lived mostly in crowded tenements, a family on each floor. The best floors, neither too far up to climb nor too close to the noisy, smelly street, were occupied by those who could pay higher rent – which meant that classes were divided as much by altitude as by topography, and were in daily, unavoidable contact. This was the world James Aitken was born into, and where he spent what would turn out to be most of his life.

Aitken was hardly at the bottom of the city's social ladder. George Aitken, his father, was a locksmith, one of the more complex and delicate metal trades. What confirmed George's respectability, and showed that he was relatively prosperous, was his status as a burgess and a deacon of the metalworkers' guild (known as the Hammermen), with a vote in the election for Lord Provost, Edinburgh's equivalent of a mayor. Such status made George Aitken part of the city's labour elite, sitting high above the ranks of apprentices and journeymen who hoped to one day become burgesses themselves. But it still left him beneath the merchants and professionals who worked mostly with pen and ink, let alone the rich men who need do no work at all.[4]

James was pampered as much as a young boy could be in a working household in the eighteenth century. When he looked back on his childhood, he wondered if his father's love had helped to make him who he was. 'By gratifying all my desires', he speculated, perhaps George had unwittingly cultivated his son's 'stubborn and obdurate disposition'.[5] Used to getting what he wanted, and to being loved by those around him, James grew up without often feeling the sting of adversity. Then his father died. At seven, he felt loss and powerlessness for the first time. Perhaps it was that, as much as the pampering, that shaped the way he would later approach the world.

His father's death was linked directly to the thing that really changed Aitken's life – his admission to Heriot's School two years later, at the age of nine. Back then, Heriot's was called a hospital, and it was in fact a kind of orphanage. It admitted only the children of burgesses, where their surviving families could not afford to educate them. Pupils lived together in the school's elegant sandstone quadrangle, 'more proper for the residence of a great king than the habitation of a few poor and needy orphans', as one baffled observer put it.[6] Indeed, the buildings were too grand in scale to house the few children the school could afford to feed and teach. Only a small number were admitted each year, while the rest of the space was rented out to Edinburgh shopkeepers. Aitken was one of the lucky ones.

---

4 For George Aitken, see the minute books of the Incorporation of Hammermen, 1739–1747 and 1747–1765, Edinburgh City Archive. On the Scottish working class in general, see W. Hamish Fraser, *Conflict and Class: Scottish Workers 1700–1838* (John Donald Publishers, 1988).

5 [James Aitken,] *Life of James Aitken* (Winchester, 1777), p. 12.

6 William Maitland, *The History of Edinburgh, from Its Foundation to the Present Time* (Edinburgh, 1753), p. 446, quoted in Jessica Warner, *John the Painter: The First Modern Terrorist* (Profile, 2004), p. 23.

At Heriot's, Aitken was taught to read and write, and to appreciate the classics. He called it 'a liberal education', one that included 'the heroes of antiquity' and the histories of Rome and Greece, as well as the principles of mathematics and the emerging natural sciences.[7] Basic literacy was widespread among the urban working class of eighteenth-century Britain. Men like Aitken's father could read a broadside or a hymnal and sign their names to a contract or petition. What Heriot's offered its boys was more than that, though. It was an education that, in most parts of the country, was reserved for gentlemen – one that taught its pupils to take their own minds seriously, and to have confidence in their judgements of the world.

Some of the boys at Heriot's would be picked out for further study at the University of Edinburgh. From there, with luck and a good patron, they might become part of the intellectual firmament of the Scottish Enlightenment. Or they might go on to professional careers in medicine or law. Aitken's schooling thus presented him with a new range of possible futures, including a life of status and comfort far beyond what he had known before. At Heriot's, in short, Aitken became ambitious. As his knowledge and understanding of the world grew, so did his hopes and expectations for himself.

Mostly, though, Aitken simply loved to read. He read the works of Voltaire 'with uncommon satisfaction', knowing that he should derive from the French *philosophe* 'the principles of religion and politics'. Most of all, he loved adventure stories 'of the marvellous kind', stories of 'the desperate expeditions and engagements of brave men . . . by land and sea'.[8] Homer and Virgil's epic poetry would fit this bill – so would novels by the likes of Daniel Defoe and Tobias Smollett, the very ones that Voltaire parodied in his *Candide*, published in 1759. Their picaresque heroes, sometimes brave and nearly always desperate, frequently overcame their own unfortunate beginnings to travel the world and encounter its marvels. These were not stories of virtue and honest toil, but of luck, daring, and

---

7 [Aitken,] *Life*, pp. 12, 14.
8 Ibid., p. 14.

flexible morality. In spite of his schoolmasters' warnings, Aitken drank their lessons in.

Edinburgh continued to thrive during the six years Aitken was at Heriot's. It may have been outpaced commercially by western port cities like Glasgow, but it remained at the centre of Scotland's intellectual and professional life – and its politics, such as they were. Aitken, though, increasingly dreamed of the world beyond the city's confines. When he stood to be counted every morning in the central quadrangle, he could stare up at carvings that depicted the four continents: Asia, Africa, Europe, and America. In 1764, the school bought two globes, along with new books on geography and navigation. Long before he really got to leave, Aitken's imagination had begun to rove.

As the new books and globes at Heriot's suggested, James Aitken was not the only one whose horizons were expanding. From 1754 to 1763, Britain's engagement in the Seven Years War made Scotland an increasingly integral part of a truly global empire. As Scots looked to the future, they also looked outwards to places like India and North America. There, their relationship to British power promised adventure and opportunity.

One straightforward Scottish contribution to the empire was manpower. With the internal threat of Jacobite rebellion uprooted in the wake of '45, the British Army began to see Scotland – and especially the Highlands – as a fertile recruiting ground for its armed forces. William Pitt, who had led most of the conduct of the war from Westminster, later recalled that he had seen the value in the highlanders, a 'hardy and intrepid race of men'. They in turn, he said, had 'fought with valour and conquered . . . in every part of the world'.[9] Service in the British Army, in

9 William Pitt, Lord Chatham, in Parliament, 14 January 1766, quoted in T.M. Devine, 'Soldiers of Empire, 1750–1914', in John M. MacKenzie and T.M. Devine, eds, *Scotland and the British Empire* (Oxford University Press, 2011), p. 181. See also the work of Andrew MacKillop, especially 'Military Scotland in the Age of Proto-Globalization, c.1690 to c.1815', in David Forsyth and Wendy Ugolini, eds, *A Global Force: War, Identities, and Scotland's Diaspora* (Edinburgh University Press, 2016), pp. 13–31.

distinctive local regiments, was a way of reconstructing a Scottish identity and sense of pride. It was also, of course, a route out of a region devastated by imperial reprisals and squeezed by rent-raising landlords.

Scotland provided officers as well as men. In fact, it was overrepresented in comparison with England (though not Ireland) – about a quarter of all officers were Scottish, including in the forces of the East India Company. On this score, the rebellion seemed to have hardly any impact. John Murray, who, on his father's death in 1756, became the Earl of Dunmore, had been a page to Charles Stuart during the uprising a decade earlier. But he fought in France as a captain during the Seven Years War. By the time Aitken arrived in Virginia in 1773, Dunmore was governor of the colony. A network of powerful relations explains his success, but there were many less high-flying Scottish officers from humbler backgrounds. Like the rank-and-file soldiers, service to the empire took them around the world.

By the 1760s, there was two-way traffic between Scotland and the colonies in North America. Britain's victory over the French and their Indigenous allies, the conquest of Canada and assertion of hegemony across the eastern portion of the continent, made settlement there once more an attractive option for those who sought abundant land and the freedom that came with greater distance from established order. A wave of migration in the wake of the Seven Years War saw thousands of Scots (as well as many more Scots-Irish from the Ulster counties) cross the Atlantic for the colonies, many of them on their way to backcountry and frontier zones. Such migrants were not always warmly welcomed by existing colonists, yet they contributed to the booming settler population, and to the imperial dreams of American land speculators.

Travelling in the other direction were the soldiers returning home, whose stories helped shape Scottish understanding of the global British Empire and its enemies. Their experience of warfare, and of army life, was often grim. But they also had tales to tell that might fit Aitken's definition of the marvellous – stories of wide oceans and far-off lands, strange animals and even stranger people.

No one had the knack for telling such tales quite like Peter Williamson. Born near the eastern Scottish port city of Aberdeen in 1730, Williamson crossed the Atlantic at the age of thirteen – cajoled onto a ship while he was walking by the dockside and taken to the colonies as an indentured servant. Surviving a shipwreck off the New Jersey coast, young Williamson was sold in Philadelphia for seven years of labour. He spent the rest of his teenage years working on a Pennsylvania farm. But next came the more exciting, partly fabricated chapter of the tale. In 1754, soon after he had got his freedom, married, and set up his own farm, Williamson was captured by an unknown band of Native Americans. When he escaped several months later, he found that his wife had died, and that was when he joined up with the British Army. Fighting in New York and Pennsylvania, he was finally captured again – this time, by the French – at the fort of Oswego on Lake Ontario. It was a French ship that brought him back across the Atlantic, landing at Plymouth as part of a prisoner exchange in 1757. From there, he began the journey back to Aberdeen.

Williamson first came to Edinburgh in 1758, having been expelled from Aberdeen by city authorities unhappy with his claims about the trade in underage servants. He brought with him copies of his book, *French and Indian Cruelty*, which had first been published in York the year before as he made his way north. For a few years, Williamson toured Scotland, selling the book and performing his story of adventure and captivity, often dressed in an improvised Indian regalia involving feathers and a tomahawk pipe. In 1760, he settled in Edinburgh and established the American Coffeehouse, presumably with the profits from his book tour. A life-size wooden figure of a Mohawk chief stood by the door, alongside a sign that promised encounters with 'the other world'.[10]

Needless to say, this was the kind of thing Aitken adored. Williamson's stories came straight from the adventure novels of the eighteenth century, fitting right in with – and, in fact, inspired by – other semi-fictional accounts of life on the margins of empire. As he grew famous and (almost) respectable, Williamson came to represent a combined social

---

10 Timothy J. Shannon, *Indian Captive, Indian King: Peter Williamson in America and Britain* (Harvard University Press, 2018), pp. 216–17; see also Shannon, 'King of the Indians: The Hard and Curious Career of Peter Williamson', *William and Mary Quarterly* 66, no. 1 (January 2009), pp. 3–44.

and geographical mobility within the expanding British world. Yet his tale of child kidnapping and indenture was also a reminder of how brutal that world was, and how much it relied on exploitation both at home and overseas. Williamson and others like him could have framed themselves as victims of the British Empire. Mostly, though, they were its enthusiastic champions.

For most Britons, Scots very much included, the Seven Years War appeared as a triumph of martial prowess, imperial strategy, and divine providence in favour of the true, Protestant religion. Its ending, however, would prove to be the starting point for serious divisions in the empire, and among the nations of the British Isles.

Central to the conflict at the war's end was a Scotsman named John Stuart, Earl of Bute. He was tutor to the Prince of Wales – the future George III – and a close confidant of his mother, Princess Augusta. When the prince became king at the age of twenty-two in late 1760, Bute thrust himself to the foreground of the political scene. Appointed to the cabinet that spring, he succeeded in ousting first Pitt, the architect of Britain's war strategy, and then the prime minister, the Duke of Newcastle. With the new king's firm backing, Bute took over as prime minister and set about negotiating peace with France. Predictably, these manoeuvres caused outrage among Pitt's friends. Given Pitt's glorification in the press, though, discontent also spread well beyond the Westminster elite. By 1763, Bute had become an emblem of unwelcome Scottish power and its threat to English liberty.

Bute's treaty with France – which gave back several Caribbean islands under British occupation, while bringing into the empire the substantial Catholic population of French Canada – was denounced by Pitt and his supporters. It was the 'ambition of the Scotch', as one particularly forthright critic put it, 'to rule the poor English with a rod of iron . . . [and] to cram an inadequate peace down their throats.'[11] Bute was out of

---

11 [Anon.,] *The Contrast: With Corrections and Restorations. And an Introductory Dissertation on the Origin of the Feuds and Animosities in the State* (London, 1765), p. 143. On the reaction to Bute among the British and colonial public, see Tim Worth, 'Transatlantic Scotophobia: Nation, Empire, and Anti-Scottish Sentiment in England and America, 1760–1783' (PhD diss., University of Southampton, 2016).

office by that summer, but the political waves made by his short tenure would continue to break over the coming decade. One of its enduring outcomes was to once more cast the Scots as friends of unrestricted royal power, a legend that was thoroughly established in America by the eve of the revolution.

With no parliament of its own, and an administration dominated by a handful of well-connected noblemen, Scotland in James Aitken's time was certainly no hotbed of radical politics. But there was one institution within which an ideal of ordinary people's rights was nurtured, and a rhetoric of moral opposition to oppression was articulated. Strange as it may seem, that institution was the Church of Scotland.

The status and structure of the Scottish Church had been a matter of sharp, sometimes violent contestation since the Reformation. It was the Scottish Covenanters who, in forcefully rejecting royal control of Church doctrine and the hierarchy of Crown-appointed bishops, helped spark the wars of revolution and dynastic struggle that burned through the British Isles in the mid-seventeenth century. After the revolution that put William and Mary on the throne in 1688, the Crown at last backed down from trying to impose its bishops and endorsed a Presbyterian structure – churches were led by local elders, and therefore subject to a form of community governance rather than top-down rule. Sharing the same Calvinist roots as many New England churches, this tradition of popular power made the Church of Scotland something rather different to its counterpart south of the border.

As Scotland transformed in the eighteenth century, with the union of 1707 and the growing influence of English capital, disputes within the Church grew to reflect prevailing social forces. Moderates among the clergy allied themselves to Scotland's elite, advocating a progressive, tempered Christianity fit for a modern, commercial society. Others – known as the popular party – resisted this move, defending a more doctrinally rigid, evangelical faith. They looked with suspicion on changes to the countryside economy, and they objected to landlords' attempts to gain more power over Church appointments.

With widespread support among ordinary congregants, the popular party was an expression of both conservative reaction and radical dissent. Its ministers were among the key opposition spokesmen of the age.[12]

Conservative as it was in some ways, the popular party was by no means parochial. Rather, it was well connected in the transatlantic evangelical movement that had flourished since the so-called Great Awakening of the 1730s and 1740s. Popular clergy saw the British Empire as an instrument for the global triumph of Protestant Christianity. They also, like many religious dissenters before them, looked to the colonies in North America as a haven for oppressed Europeans. As Britain's imperial crisis emerged during the 1760s, in the wake of the Seven Years War, their sense of attachment to the colonists only grew – deepening, in turn, their stance of opposition to the metropolitan regime.

By then, John Witherspoon was one of the most prominent advocates of the popular cause. The son of a minister in East Lothian, and a graduate of Edinburgh University, he served congregations in Ayrshire and Paisley in the western lowlands – the region most closely connected with the transatlantic trade. In 1753, he published a popular satire attacking the moderates for prioritising 'the present life' over the heavenly afterlife, and for their tendency to prefer clergy who were 'very unacceptable to the common people'.[13] True religious doctrine, he contended, was something that any man could understand. In 1766, Witherspoon's fame as an evangelical hardliner got the attention of the College of New Jersey (later to become Princeton University), which offered him its presidency. Sailing for America two years later, he soon

12 See Ned Landsman, 'Witherspoon and the Problem of Provincial Identity in Scottish Evangelical Culture', in Richard Sher and Jeffrey Smitten, eds, *Scotland and America in the Age of Enlightenment* (Princeton University Press, 1990), pp. 29–45; Robert Kent Donovan, 'The Popular Party of the Church of Scotland and the American Revolution', in Sher and Smitten, *Scotland and America*, pp. 81–99; Landsman, 'The Provinces and the Empire: Scotland, the American Colonies and the Development of British Provincial Identity', in Lawrence Stone, ed., *An Imperial State at War: Britain from 1689 to 1815* (Routledge, 1994), pp. 258–87.

13 [John Witherspoon,] *Ecclesiastical Characteristics* (Edinburgh, 1753), quoted in Landsman, 'Witherspoon and Provincial Identity', p. 35.

took up the cause of colonial liberty, becoming a signatory to the Declaration of Independence.

Witherspoon left Scotland for America with a good deal of reluctance, but once there he did not hesitate to recommend emigration to other Scots. Investing in land schemes, he had a financial motive to encourage settlement. But he also believed that the New World had become a better home than the Old for liberty and true religion. Increasing numbers of Scots thought the same.

While Witherspoon served in the west and then America, his friend and close contemporary John Erskine was his counterpart at the heart of Scotland's capital. Called to Greyfriar's Church, Edinburgh, in 1758, he preached there for the next four decades, operating as a leader of the popular party even while he maintained friendships with the city's moderate intellectual elite. It was Erskine whose preaching young Aitken was subjected to as a boy at Heriot's, sitting in the loft built specially for them when Greyfriars was reconfigured in 1722. If he listened at all, Aitken would have heard much praise of simple, honest piety, and subtle condemnation of the sophistry that veiled corruption.

Aitken was out of Heriot's, but still in Edinburgh, when Erskine took up the topic of the American crisis most directly and publicly. In his 1769 address and pamphlet, *Shall I Go to War with My American Brethren?*, he described the colonies as 'a seat of liberty and true religion', which he loved as dearly as Britain itself. Still more provocatively, Erskine concurred with the colonists' argument that the parliament in London had no right to levy taxes on them. By persisting in denying their claims, he argued, 'we may drive them into measures, ruinous both to themselves and to us'. Britain should not rely on the colonies' lack of armed strength, for 'a people thus roughly enraged, will soon find themselves a method'. Those resisting despotism had done so before.[14]

When Aitken said later that he had been raised 'in the persuasion of a protestant dissenter', there can be little doubt that what he meant was the evangelical Presbyterianism of Witherspoon and Erskine's popular

---

14 John Erskine, *Shall I Go to War with My American Brethren?* (London, 1769), pp. 3, 19, 20.

party.[15] Although they preached within an established Church, they did so in a dissenting spirit – one closely matching that of their cousins in America and among dissenting sects in England. In an otherwise quiescent Scotland, their voices spoke loudly in the name of righteous opposition. If, at the time, Aitken paid them less attention than he did men like Peter Williamson, it would not be long before he had cause to remember what they preached.

For six years, Aitken lived and studied at Heriot's. Had he done well, his next step might have been university. But Aitken came from the poorer end of the school's social scale, and its governors' assessment was not kind to him. Like most of the boys, his education was destined to continue as an apprentice – bound to a master of a particular trade, who would pass on his skills in exchange for five years' labour and an upfront payment from the school. According to the story Aitken later told, it was his 'natural taste for drawing' that determined the trade chosen for him.[16] It was also this trade that gave him the nickname by which he was known in all the nation's newspapers a few years later: John the Painter.

Painting meant more than simply whitewashing a house wall, a task that required no special training. It began with mixing the paints themselves, a process that demanded equal parts aesthetic and scientific understanding. As for the application, the devil was in the detail, with drawing a crucial step in composition and planning. Painters were expected to be able to paint signs for shops and public houses, as well as the intricate patterns of colour that some citizens preferred. In Edinburgh's Old Town, as one visitor remarked, the buildings were truly riotous: 'Each story, perhaps, from top to bottom, is chequered with ten thousand different forms and colours.'[17] Such displays needed regular upkeep, as well as updating when shops changed their function.

---

15 [Aitken,] *Life*, p. 12.

16 Ibid., p. 13.

17 Edward Topham, *Letters from Edinburgh, Written in the Years 1774 and 1775* (Dublin, n.d.), p. 45, quoted in Warner, *John the Painter*, p. 36.

In general, painting came low on the scale of prestigious or lucrative trades in the mid-eighteenth century. For one thing, ready-mixed paints were becoming available, undermining the market for painters' skills. Yet in 1767, when Aitken's time at Heriot's came to an end, there was good reason for a painter to take on a new apprentice. That year, construction began on what would become known as the New Town – the spacious and elegant new quarter, to the city's north, which was soon to house its monied and professional elite. Naturally, the style of the New Town was quite different to the Old, but painters were still needed to mix the more understated colours that were deemed tasteful for modern interiors.

An apprentice's life was not often easy – he was, in effect, a servant, and expected to work uncomplainingly at any task he was given. Aitken, though, remembered his old master as 'indulgent'. What was more, moving back in with his mother Magdalen, he returned to having 'all my desires gratified at home'. When he was not working at his trade, Aitken spent most of the next five years reading. His body remained in Edinburgh, within a few miles of where he was born. But his mind continued to go everywhere, thirsting for marvellous adventures and, perhaps, 'some great achievement'.[18] By the time he completed his apprenticeship in 1772, Aitken was more than ready to get out of Edinburgh. He also knew exactly what he wanted to do next.

'I had very early contracted an itch for the service', Aitken recalled on the eve of his hanging five years later.[19] To fight in the British Army was a common enough dream among Scots of his generation – and, if some heard tales such as Peter Williamson's and recognised the horror and hardship of soldiering on the borders of empire, there were plenty who chose to focus on the glory. In any case, what Aitken wanted was not the life of a common soldier, but an officer's commission. That would place him among the ranks of gentlemen, and equal enough to many a younger son of the Scottish nobility. It would sate, for the time being, the ambition for status and advancement that he had contracted

18 [Aitken,] *Life*, pp. 13–14.
19 Ibid., p. 14.

at Heriot's, as well as the lust for adventure. To become an officer would do his father proud.

The problem was that a commission was no easy thing to come by. It required two things – friends and money – that the Aitkens could by no means count on. True, James's mother had been able to call upon patrons in the city to help him get into Heriot's. The wealthy merchant's widow Sarah Sandilands, then in her late sixties, had presented the nine-year-old Aitken to the school's governors. Eleven years later, James turned to his mother for help 'in importuning my friends and relations to serve me' in the search for a commission.[20] But it was not to be. Most of the Scots who sought commissions were far better placed than him, and even then, they sometimes served years in the ranks before their benefactors could secure one.

The year 1772 was also a bad moment to be asking for favours in Edinburgh. A severe economic slowdown had begun even before word of James Fordyce's spectacular bankruptcy reached the city that June. The Ayr Bank – with branches in Edinburgh and elsewhere – collapsed within a fortnight of the news, leaving a trail of distressed creditors and partners in its wake. As the vanguard of a proudly commercial society, Edinburgh's elite was deeply enmeshed with the country's financial industry. Work on the New Town meant to house them came to a sudden halt, who knew when to resume. 'The year 1772 will ever be remembered as a year of confusion, dismay, and distress', wrote James Boswell. 'All Scotland has been shaken by a kind of commercial earthquake.'[21] If there was anyone who might have helped Aitken to purchase his commission, they were scarcely in the mood to do so that summer.

Thwarted and frustrated, Aitken cast about for some other plan. There seemed to be nothing for him in Edinburgh – not even, for the present, much by way of painting work. He might have chosen emigration to America, as many of his fellow Scots were doing, but the notion of

---

20 Ibid., p. 15.

21 James Boswell, *Reflections on the Late Alarming Bankruptcies in Scotland* (Edinburgh, 1772), p. 1. See Henry Hamilton, 'The Failure of the Ayr Bank, 1772', *Economic History Review* 8, no. 3 (1956), pp. 405–17.

backcountry farming did not interest the lifelong city-dweller. Really only one obvious option remained. The road to London was one many an ambitious lad had taken before him. That summer, Aitken 'embarked for London with all the monies I could scrape together, not doubting but I should get into some creditable employ before it was all spent'.[22] He never again set foot north of the border.

---

22 [Aitken,] *Life*, p. 15.

3

London

There is danger in the metropolis, and not just for newcomers like James Aitken. There, the seat of government sits next door to the centre of commerce and finance, toe to toe with the engine-rooms of trade and industry. It is a city that draws everything into itself – the power, and the money, the commodities, and most importantly the people: the ambitious artists, writers, politicians, fanatics, the merchants and adventurers, the optimists, the exiles, and the landless, out-of-work poor. A metropolis can be an overwhelming thing. It overwhelms both the provincials and the provinces, and it can even overwhelm itself. Set loose, it can become the crucible of revolution. Indeed, there were moments in the eighteenth century when that was just what London seemed to threaten, or to promise.

When Aitken arrived in 1772, there were signs all around him of that year's financial panic. Just as work had stopped on the New Town in Edinburgh, so the great speculative projects of London – most notably the Adam brothers' Adelphi building below the Strand – lay in a state of partial completion. Robert Adam was a Scotsman who had started his career in London with the help of the Earl of Bute, when it seemed as if the Scots were everywhere. In 1768, Adam entered Parliament as MP for Kinross, and, in the same year, he began work on the new riverside townhouses that were now stalled, leaving builders and craftsmen suddenly in limbo. When merchants and banks failed, the effects spread quickly to ordinary citizens. Construction trades, including Aitken's house painting, were often the first hit when money was suddenly tight and investors pulled back on their commitments.

New journeymen arriving in the city might expect to be at the bottom of the list for what work was available. The city's working class had an internal hierarchy that, in some respects at least, subordinated footloose journeymen like Aitken to the established, independent masters of their trades – and placed both above those who had never learned a trade at all. At the same time, such distinctions were coming apart during the eighteenth century, as labour came to be organised more and more by the demands of capital, not workers and their traditions.

Organised workers could fight back, as coal-heavers did at Wapping in 1768 when an agent undercut their rates by hiring lower-paid men. They besieged him in his own public house, firing pistols and muskets and declaring they would 'cut him to pieces and hang him on his sign'.[1] The next year, silk-weavers in Spitalfields launched a campaign of strikes and sabotage for higher wages that soon escalated into violence, with weavers and soldiers shooting one another in the streets. Though it subsided with the execution of two ringleaders, the uprising pushed Parliament to regulate weavers' wages in a 1773 Spitalfields Act. These were just two of the 'fiercest and most memorable' clashes, in the words of horrified memoirist Horace Walpole.[2] The decade after the Seven Years War saw London's streets frequently transformed into industrial battlegrounds, as employers and entrepreneurs used new machinery and discipline to squeeze more productivity from workers even while they tried to keep wage increases below the cost of living.

Gentler forms of solidarity also continued to shape the experience of London workers. When the Scottish slater Samuel Kevan first arrived, a decade after Aitken, at the age of eighteen or nineteen, he

---

1 George Rudé, *Hanoverian London* (Sutton Publishing, 2003 [1971]), p. 197.

2 Horace Walpole, *Memoirs of the Reign of King George III*, vol. 3 (London, 1845), p. 117.

wandered around asking for help until he spotted a team working on a roof. 'Knowing them by their tools', Kevan approached the men for work, telling 'a plain tale that I was just arrived in town'. When the master slater learned that the young man had nowhere to stay, he took him home and let him sleep in his son's bed. 'I received the greatest kindness from him', Kevan later recalled, having long since settled down in the city.[3]

Aitken's own account suggests that he was just as lucky. 'On my arrival in the great metropolis,' he told the clerk who took down his life story before his hanging, 'I applied to people in the painting way, and immediately got into employ.'[4] Being Scottish seemed to cause him no more difficulty than it would Kevan, in spite of the anti-Scottish animus that riled London under Bute's premiership a decade earlier. The city's working class was cosmopolitan and multiracial, though inevitably not without some friction. Among the 750,000 Londoners were some 10,000 Black people and twice as many Irish. Less than half the city's population was actually born in London. Most, like Aitken, had to find their own way there.

It may have been that the timing worked out well for Aitken. By the end of that summer, the impact of the panic was already lessening in London – though it would cut longer and deeper in places like Virginia. Work on the Adelphi soon resumed, with the project completed by 1774. Other ongoing building work included redevelopment of the Minories, a down-at-heel street along the eastern city wall being transformed into a set of refined terraces modelled on Bath: America Square, the Crescent, and the Circus. Such projects must have created work for men like Aitken, bringing skills from Edinburgh's New Town. If he was willing to take lower rates than London house painters, and keep it quiet, all the better as far as employers were concerned.

Unlike Kevan, Aitken reached London with a little money in his pocket – enough to pay for some cheap lodgings while he found work,

---

3 Jerry White, *London in the Eighteenth Century: A Great and Monstrous Thing* (Bodley Head, 2012), p. 99.

4 [James Aitken,] *Life of James Aitken* (Winchester, 1777), p. 15.

anyway. If he had followed the advice of *The Art of Living in London: A Poem in Two Cantos*, rising early for a breakfast of gruel (strictly no tea: it took too long to prepare), eschewing the fashion for 'well dressed hair', and generally attending to his business with a will, he might have eventually carved out a meagre London life.[5] But that was not what Aitken was about. For him, arriving in 'the great metropolis' was meant to be a chance to rise.

Londoners in general had a problem with knowing their place. 'There is no distinction or subordination left', complained a character in one of the Scotsman Tobias Smollett's novels. 'The different departments of life are jumbled together', from the 'low mechanic' (artisan) to the 'pettifogger' (minor lawyer) and the 'courtier'.[6] Freedom of expression in the streets and on the waterways – rudeness that did not discriminate by rank – was a tradition dearly guarded by London's working people. No less a figure than Giacomo Casanova complained of being pelted with mud as he crossed the street in fancy clothes. Gentlemen soon learned to expect that 'the rabble' would be 'insolent and abusive'.[7]

During the 1760s, this egalitarian street spirit was increasingly politicised. As part of a coalition that also included tradesmen and merchants, London's workers came to identify themselves with a tradition of liberty that often put them at loggerheads with the imperial government and its representatives. The city became a centre of opposition thought and practice that, like other metropolitan trends, quickly radiated to provincial towns as well. By the eve of the American Revolution, there was an urban political culture throughout England that was quite accustomed to taking a stand against the ministry – and, where necessary, against Parliament itself.

---

5 [Anon.,] *The Art of Living in London: A Poem in Two Cantos* (London, 1768), p. 3.

6 Tobias Smollett, *The Expedition of Humphrey Clinker* (London, 1771), quoted in White, *London*, p. 104.

7 [Anon.,] *The London and Westminster Guide Through the Cities and Suburbs* (London, 1768), p. xxiii.

At the heart of these developments there was a single man: the controversialist, sometime demagogue, and icon of the city's truculence, John Wilkes.[8] In his forties by the time James Aitken arrived in London in 1772, and nearly at the height of his power, Wilkes was both celebrity and *cause célèbre*. He had first come to widespread attention as a backbench MP a decade earlier, when the Earl of Bute's ascent to power displaced the popular champion and victor of the Seven Years War, William Pitt. Over the next ten years, a series of conflicts saw Wilkes pitted against not only Bute but Crown and Parliament as well. By rallying behind him, Londoners affirmed their independence from all these authorities, achieving a degree of unity in popular defiance.

Wilkes's most famous piece of writing was the forty-fifth issue of his newspaper, the *North Briton*, published soon after Bute's resignation in 1763 (the name alluded to *The Briton*, a pro-Bute paper). In it, he excoriated that year's unpopular treaty with France as well as the new tax on cider, declaring that 'the honour of the crown [was] sunk even to prostitution', sold out to the 'tools of corruption and despotism' that constituted the new ministry under George Grenville.[9] Within days, so-called general warrants were issued for the arrest of all those involved in the publication. Wilkes spent a week in the Tower of London facing charges of seditious libel before the case against him was dismissed on the grounds of parliamentary immunity.

Government did not, however, let the matter lie. The next year, charges against Wilkes were revived – over the *North Briton*, plus a salacious poem he had toyed with printing. Fleeing to Paris, Wilkes remained there for the next four years, until in 1768 he chose to roll the dice on re-entering public life in London. Duly elected as a new MP for Middlesex – the county surrounding London and Westminster's formal boundaries – Wilkes was prevented from taking his seat by a decision of Parliament itself. Three times he was expelled from the legislature, and three times

---

8 In addition to George Rudé, *Wilkes and Liberty: A Social Study of 1763–1774* (Oxford University Press, 1962), see Peter D.G. Thomas, *John Wilkes: A Friend to Liberty* (Oxford University Press, 1996); and Robin Eagles, *Champion of English Freedom: The Life of John Wilkes, MP and Lord Mayor of London* (Amberley Publishing, 2024).

9 [John Wilkes,] *North Briton*, no. 45 (London, 1763), n.p.

the people of Middlesex insisted on voting him back in, only to have their will overturned again. Now he was a champion not only of the freedom of the press, but of the rights of voters and for parliamentary reform.

In the course of his campaigns, Wilkes had long since fallen out with the leaders of the parliamentary Whig Party – most importantly William Pitt, newly ennobled as the Earl of Chatham, who had retaken the office of prime minister from 1766 to 1768. Splitting off from the loyal opposition that took place within the privileged spaces of the Palace of Westminster, Wilkes's cause represented a new kind of popular opposition, uniting the disenfranchised and the disaffected in and beyond the capital. Never exactly an idealist or a revolutionary, Wilkes nonetheless became a mascot for many who were excluded from the oligarchic structure of British politics.

For Londoners, what this meant was a redoubled sense of political confidence. 'There is not a citizen,' sneered one critic in 1766, 'but what is capable of filling the first offices of government. The veriest drudge, who now wears a leathern apron, can tell how far a secretary of state's power ought to extend.'[10] Those who qualified as gentlemen and took part in polite society were not at all accustomed to having their leadership of the country and its empire systematically questioned, or to their working-class neighbours raising their voices on questions of politics and law. Yet both phenomena were increasingly commonplace by the early 1770s, especially in London.

In Scotland, the closest thing Aitken had known to this confident working-class politics was the popular party in the Church of Scotland clergy – and that was a rather different proposition. Men like John Witherspoon and John Erskine were university-educated ministers speaking from the pulpit and the press. Their willingness to articulate outspoken opposition and to mount a critique of the dominant trends in Scottish society was undoubtedly a challenge to the country's elite. But what Aitken encountered in London was something else. United, the city's working people were a force that established authorities could not

10 John Sainsbury, *Disaffected Patriots: London Supporters of Revolutionary America, 1769–1782* (McGill Queens University Press, 1987), p. 23.

control or muzzle. By shutting Wilkes out of Parliament, those authorities only emphasised the gulf between the class they represented and the much more numerous one they did not. For some, at least, their actions helped bring the entire system into question.

While John Wilkes's movement – and its cry for 'Wilkes and Liberty!' – emerged in London from 1763, a crisis was growing in the administration of Britain's empire. The timing, of course, was no coincidence.

When William Pitt was ousted from the cabinet and, shortly afterwards, the Earl of Bute took over as prime minister, it signalled a major shift in the British government's approach to colonial rule. Retrenchment and consolidation – some might say austerity – became the order of the day. Colonists' westward encroachment onto Native American land was supposed to cease. Regular soldiers were posted to the continent, partly to make sure it did. To help pay for them, new taxes were imposed directly by Parliament. Enforcement of the customs regime was ramped up, forcing the colonists to pay duties they had been avoiding for generations. Suddenly, the distant imperial government felt much more present in many Americans' lives, right when a post-war economic slowdown was already pinching. The result was a decade of evolving resistance and intermittent rebellion.

One example of the shifting colonial temper could be found in the backcountry and frontier zones. There, the new policy of seeking stable peace with Indigenous nations – represented by the Proclamation Line that set a western limit to white land claims – led to frustration among settlers who expected to be able to take frontier land with impunity. Settler anger exploded into violence on several occasions in the decade after 1763, most often against Indigenous people themselves, but sometimes directed at imperial authorities as well. Movements of settlers known as Regulators pitted themselves against what they saw as corruption and tyranny emanating from the centres of commerce and power to the east.

But the most direct resistance to British policy came from the seaport towns and cities themselves. When Parliament passed the Stamp Act in

1765, taxing newspapers and legal documents among various other paper products, colonists poured into the streets to protest, hanging effigies of the tax collectors and breaking the windows of their houses. In Boston that August, a crowd destroyed the mansion that belonged to Massachusetts's governor, Thomas Hutchinson. In Charleston, armed protesters with their faces blackened broke into the home of local slave trader and politician Henry Laurens, searching for the stamps that would be used to enforce the Act. In New York, a crowd gathered to menace the fort that held the stamps, building a bonfire of furniture from the commander's house and even the lieutenant governor's coach.[11]

In these and other crowd actions that punctuated the next decade of imperial crisis, workers were at the forefront of the struggle. Artisans, labourers, and sailors came together in colonial cities in defiance of imperial policies that dampened trade, threatened their livelihoods, and undermined colonial self-government.[12] These complaints also aligned working-class protesters with local merchants and professionals – men such as Samuel Adams and John Hancock, who became the best-known leaders of the anti-ministerial resistance in Boston, for example. This cross-class alliance in colonial cities closely resembled the one forged around Wilkes in London at the same time. In both cases, workers and the well-to-do found common ground in their exclusion from the imperial oligarchy, and their sense that decisions were being made against their shared interests.

By the end of the 1760s, a close collaboration had been formed between the colonial resistance movement and Wilkites in the metropolis. While Wilkes himself was in prison, during 1768, having returned from Paris to serve out his sentence for seditious libel, he received gifts and

<hr>

11 David Duncan Wallace, *The Life of Henry Laurens, with a Sketch of the Life of Lieutenant-Colonel John Laurens* (G.P. Putnam's Sons, 1915), pp. 117–19; F.L. Engelman, 'Cadwallader Colden and the New York Stamp Act Riots', *William and Mary Quarterly* 10, no. 4 (October 1953), pp. 560–78.

12 Jesse Lemisch, 'Jack Tar in the Streets: Merchant Seamen in the Politics of Revolutionary America', *William and Mary Quarterly* 25, no. 3 (July 1968), pp. 371–407; Gary Nash, *The Urban Crucible: The Northern Seaports and the Origins of the American Revolution* (Harvard University Press, 1979); Benjamin Carp, *Rebels Rising: Cities and the American Revolution* (Oxford University Press, 2007).

compliments from American admirers. Responding to the Sons of Liberty in Boston he assured them, 'You have many warm friends here, who will never give up your cause.'[13] Sympathetic London papers like the *Public Advertiser* reprinted news from the colonies, while booksellers stocked anti-ministerial American authors such as James Otis and John Dickinson. City officials began including pleas on the colonists' behalf in their petitions to the Westminster government.

Some Americans worked directly to nurture and influence Londoners' commitment to their rights and autonomy within the British Empire. The most prolific was the young Arthur Lee, son of a slave-owning Virginia family who had been schooled at Eton and the University of Edinburgh. Arriving in London in 1768, Lee wrote incessantly for the press, while also studying law at Lincoln's Inn and working his way into the city's political life. He was active in the Society for the Support of the Bill of Rights, a pro-Wilkes club that included many leading London radicals, but he also used his elite credentials to cultivate friendships with Whig parliamentarians like the Earl of Shelburne.

Lee's basic political strategy was to drum home the unity of principle between the Wilkite and American causes. In a typically fiery polemic from 1770, he explained that while the voters of Middlesex had been 'unjustly and arbitrarily deprived of a representative' when Wilkes was refused his seat in Parliament, 'the people of America . . . are deprived of every representative'. What was more, he continued, anyone could see that this was only the beginning. Once 'arbitrary rule' was established in the colonies, it would 'speedily traverse the ocean, and finally fix itself in England'.[14]

---

13 Sainsbury, *Disaffected Patriots*, p. 33. For connections between Wilkes's support and the colonial movement, in addition to Sainsbury, see Pauline Maier, 'John Wilkes and American Disillusionment with Britain', *William and Mary Quarterly* 20, no. 3 (July 1963), pp. 373–95; Micah Alpaugh, *Friends of Freedom: The Rise of Social Movements in the Age of Atlantic Revolutions* (Cambridge University Press, 2022), pp. 70–94.

14 Junius Americanus [Arthur Lee], *Gazetteer and New Daily Advertiser*, 3 January 1770, p. 1. On Lee, see A.R. Riggs, 'Arthur Lee, a Radical Virginian in London, 1768–1776', *Virginia Magazine of History and Biography* 78, no. 3 (July 1970), pp. 268–70.

Months after those words were published, British soldiers guarding the Customs House in Boston fired into a crowd of protesters who were shouting and throwing snowballs at them. Three Americans died on the scene, including the mixed-race sailor Crispus Attucks; two more died of their wounds later. Dubbed a 'bloody massacre' in Paul Revere's famous and popular engraving, the incident only served to remind Wilkites of the similarity between the two movements. Less than two years earlier, at least six people had been killed by soldiers trying to disperse a crowd of Wilkes's supporters outside the prison he was being held in. Violent repression by the British state was never confined to just one side of the Atlantic.

What did the twenty-year-old James Aitken, freshly arrived from Edinburgh in the summer of 1772, make of the Wilkite movement and its solidarity with the American cause? As an avid reader, he might easily have been captivated by pamphlets and newspaper essays that warned of the growing tyranny of British government. In conversation with his fellow tradesmen, he would certainly have come to know about John Wilkes's travails with the ministry. His encounter with London's politically confident working class could well have been a moment for his own political awakening. In truth, though, he showed little interest in any of that.

Aitken had not come to London to engage in politics. For the first time in his life, he was his own man – no matron, master, or mother to keep an eye on where he went, who he spent time with, or how late he got back home at night. More than that, he was no longer in Edinburgh, where every inch of the city's cramped streets was already familiar, and networks of acquaintances were never far away. In the metropolis, Aitken had a new world to discover. He was, in a sense, vulnerable. But he was also young, strong enough, and by no means slow-witted. He was ready for adventure – and that was something London could provide.

Innocent provincial ensnared by the wily urbanite, country mouse duped by city rat was already an ancient story when the Roman Empire was at its height 1,000 years before. Plenty of the kinds of novels

Aitken himself read employed the trope, and in the eighteenth century the city as corrupting force was a theme of both religious and secular philosophising. Unfortunately for Aitken, this did not mean it was just the stuff of fiction or social theory. Real people arriving in the city, and especially the ones whose pockets were not completely empty, really could find themselves the targets of fair-weather friends. Without meaning to, these people could be 'led into all manner of vice and debauchery'.[15] That was Aitken's story, anyway, and he was sticking to it.

Two obvious forms of vice and debauchery presented themselves in every similar account from the era, and each of them took on a range of forms to suit all tastes and, more importantly, all pockets.

The first of these vices was gambling. If rich men were to be found throwing away their fortunes at the racetrack or the card-tables of convivial gentlemen's clubs, there were no fewer opportunities for workers like Aitken to lose their pay on the roll of a die or the toss of a coin. In *The Art of Living in London*, the poet explained how some men sat outside pubs, ostensibly trying and failing to 'chuck a shilling' into a glass. When a passing mark – 'unpractised in the rule / which sharpers hourly use to gull the fool' – proposed a bet, the silver miraculously went straight in.[16] Other, more complex games might draw someone in deeper. Patient, careful sharpers could string a mark out for weeks before he was bled dry.

Just as ubiquitous on London's streets, the second vice was sex. Although Covent Garden, Drury Lane, and the Strand were the most well-known centres of prostitution, plenty of commentators claimed to see sex work everywhere, entrapping 'youths' and 'thoughtless virgins', as *The Art of Living* had it.[17] Expensive courtesans catered to profligate nobles and prosperous merchants, but encounters were also available much more cheaply, often in alleys and bushes under cover of night. Women in London's sex trade belonged to the city's working class, along

---

15 [Aitken,] *Life*, p. 15.
16 [Anon.,] *Art of Living*, p. 14.
17 Ibid., p. 17.

with many more who brought in wages, supported families, or simply earned their keep as domestic servants. Like other workers, they were ruthlessly exploited by the system they were part of.

Having started this slide into debauchery, neglecting his house painting work and joining up with a gang of 'extravagant young men', Aitken quickly found himself broke. So far, so inevitable. But it was his next move that marked out how far he was willing to go in defiance of the order and authority he had grown up with in Edinburgh. Maybe it was his childhood stubbornness coming through, or maybe the unconscious lessons he had taken from stories of desperate adventurers. Maybe it was simply the pressures of the moment. In any case, when others might have pulled back, he chose to press on – a choice that would characterise the remainder of his short life.

Here is how the story was told, in the version that eventually made it to the press. Once he ran out of money, Aitken's friends soon deserted him. He was 'in a strange country', with little prospect of advancement left. So, without really thinking more about it, he decided to become a highwayman. 'I accordingly provided myself with pistols, and without the least concern or apprehension of danger, proceeded to Finchley Common.' There, he robbed a stagecoach, several carriages, and a lone horseman, collecting 'a considerable booty' in just a few hours before midnight. When he got back to town, his old friends were rallied by this sudden accession of good fortune. Aitken was suddenly the centre of attention. His career as a criminal had begun.[18]

Highway robbery had a certain mystique in eighteenth-century Britain. Dick Turpin, its most famous real practitioner, had gone undaunted to the gallows in 1739. James Maclaine, the 'gentleman highwayman', followed him a decade later. Both were outshone, though, by their entirely fictional counterpart, the roguish Macheath, hero of *The Beggar's*

18 Ibid., pp. 15–16. On London's underworld, see Tim Hitchcock and Robert Shoemaker, *London Lives: Poverty, Crime, and the Making of a Modern City* (Cambridge University Press, 2015).

Opera. His exploits mainly involved evading the demands of various lovers as well as the authorities and the noose, but that did not prevent the character from allegedly inspiring several generations of imitators to take to the highways wielding pistols. The London magistrate John Fielding was so convinced of the popular play's effect on impressionable youth that he tried to have it banned.[19]

Like pirates, who were also the subject of literary fascination in the first half of the century, highwaymen functioned as symbols of a radical, redistributive politics – a violent rejection of legal and social orders that enriched a few at the expense of the many. The bravado of the highwayman's crime, which always involved direct encounter between thief and victim, was part of its allure. Every call to 'stand and deliver' was a temporary reversal of the day-to-day balance of power between rich and poor.[20]

For the most part, though, crime in London was both more mundane and less clearly delineated. What, other than the shifting power relation of employers and employees, distinguished the customary practice of workers taking perquisites – shipbuilders, for example, taking home the scraps of waste wood known as 'chips' – from the punishable crime of theft from the workplace? Property crime, including pickpocketing and burglary, made up the vast majority of offences prosecuted. There existed, according to authorities, a 'republic of thieves' whose citizens could scarcely be told apart from ordinary Londoners.[21] Turning a blind eye, fencing or buying stolen goods, or exchanging useful information: acts of self-interest and of solidarity helped to dissolve the criminal economy

---

19 For *The Beggar's Opera* and its influence, see John Brewer, *The Pleasures of the Imagination: English Culture in the Eighteenth Century* (Routledge, 2013 [1997]), pp. 342–60. For other crime tales, and *The Beggar's Opera* as inspiration to young highwaymen, see Andrea McKenzie, 'Making Crime Pay: Motives, Marketing Strategies, and the Printed Literature of Crime in England, 1670–1770', in Greg Smith et al., eds, *Criminal Justice in the Old World and the New* (University of Toronto Press, 1998), pp. 242–3.

20 On highway robbery in and around eighteenth-century London, see Peter Linebaugh, *The London Hanged: Crime and Civil Society in the Eighteenth Century* (Cambridge University Press, 1992), pp. 184–218.

21 White, *London*, p. 404.

into the city's ordinary life and commerce, including the gambling and prostitution that were equally ubiquitous.

James Aitken may have started his career with highway robbery, but he was soon enough reduced to 'private thefts and shop-lifting' as well. Even more than his fellow journeymen, who could earn good wages when work offered and then find themselves stretched to the bone when it did not, Aitken tacked wildly between the temporary riches of a successful score and the return to poverty that forced him back into the streets. He became increasingly concerned about the possibility of being recognised and taken by the magistrates, 'or of being betrayed by some of my companions'.[22] While many thieves and criminals refused to turn on one another, even to save their own lives, solidarity was by no means always the rule.

For those convicted of violent crimes like Aitken's, especially ones that involved substantial sums of money, the sentence was very often death by hanging. Public executions were a regular occurrence, a mixture of morbid entertainment and deliberate state terror, meant to drum home among the city's masses the inevitable outcome of disobedience to the propertied order. Brave defiance at the gallows, along with a show of generosity, could cement the legend of a famous criminal. Just as often, the condemned went to their deaths repenting, hoping for salvation in the next life, and willing to sign lurid testimony of their degradation to discourage others from their wayward paths.[23]

Swift passage to the next life at the end of a rope was not, however, the only possible outcome for an eighteenth-century convict. Those who could offer some mitigating circumstances, or whose crimes were less severe than capital offences, might be sentenced to a somewhat different kind of journey: transportation to the colonies. Designed to simultaneously purge English cities of their supposed criminal underclass, and attenuate the labour shortages complained of by New

---

22 [Aitken,] *Life*, p. 16.

23 On public execution and its functions, see Linebaugh, *London Hanged*, and Vic Gatrell, *The Hanging Tree: Execution and the English People, 1770–1868* (Oxford University Press, 1994).

World employers, the policy of transportation had begun almost as early as the first English settlement in North America.

By the mid-eighteenth century, the passage of convicts and their stories to and fro across the ocean had helped shape a well-established set of networks and associations – a criminal Atlantic, enmeshed with the wider, oceanic working class.[24] Transportation was supposed to be one-way, but there was reason to think otherwise. Plenty of stories, including *Moll Flanders* and Daniel Defoe's other popular picaresque *Colonel Jack*, depicted characters who came back from the colonies. There were at least some real cases, and who knows how many returnees were never caught. London's republic of thieves doubtless harboured citizens who claimed they had artfully escaped their punishment. Aitken must also have remembered tales such as Peter Williamson's that he heard in Edinburgh. In such accounts, the colonies might figure as places of cruelty and punishment but also of escape and opportunity.

As 1773 wore on, and his life in London grew increasingly precarious, he was prepared to revisit the New World's possibilities. Of all the places in the world that he might run to, he reckoned that America 'might turn out most to my advantage.'[25] It was also perhaps the easiest to get to, provided a traveller was willing to bargain with his liberty. Aitken was not prepared to let himself be caught by the authorities in London, and to gamble that his sentence would be transportation rather than the gallows. But by agreeing to terms of indenture – binding himself and his labour for a fixed value or length of service – he could get passage on a westbound voyage.

There were distinctions between convicts bound for the Chesapeake and those who willingly took on indentures to migrate there. For one thing, transportees could expect a lengthier term of service. Neither the forced nor voluntary white migrants, of course, were subject to the perpetual bondage and racialised oppression that was the fate of captive

---

24 For the concept of the 'criminal Atlantic' as both a social and cultural artefact, see Gwenda Morgan and Peter Rushton, *Eighteenth-Century Criminal Transportation: The Formation of the Criminal Atlantic* (Palgrave Macmillan, 2004).

25 [Aitken,] *Life*, p. 17.

Africans and their enslaved descendants – men like James Somerset, who the same summer Aitken arrived in London had been fighting in court for his right not to be carried into Caribbean slavery. Still, convict and indentured labour occupied lesser places on a scale of unfreedom for the broad Atlantic working class.

Few of those who went, even by their own free will, were truly free in the choices they made. Economic and social forces, the destruction of communities and ways of life by the advancement of capital across the British Isles, pushed men, women, and families into the decision to migrate. For Aitken, the pressure was more immediate. He had made choices, maybe bad ones, that had brought him to this situation. Now he would join a migrant flow that was reshaping the spaces of North America, both on the frontiers of white settlement and in the port cities that linked continent to continent. Having passed through the metropolis, Aitken was about to experience the imperial periphery.

4

Philadelphia

James Aitken was in North America for roughly eighteen months. Most of that time he likely spent in Philadelphia. The largest city in the colonies, it was also among the easiest to reach from Aitken's point of arrival in Virginia. When he was questioned at his trial about his time in America, Aitken gave answers that convinced the court he knew the city well. Of course, Philadelphia was no London or Edinburgh. Its population was not much over half that of Scotland's capital, tiny compared with the metropolis. Its grid-pattern streets hinted at utopian aspirations born out of the conflagration of the seventeenth century. But it was city-like enough to feel familiar. Crowded, diverse, and full of immigrants, it was as good a place as any for a runaway like Aitken to try to begin a new life.

For many of the new arrivals, Philadelphia was just a place for passing through, before the real journey began – into the west, in search of land and freedom. Scotch-Irish and German migrants crossed the ocean to move into the hills and valleys of the Appalachians, extending the ragged edges of white settlement. As these invaders' presence led to frequent violent confrontations with Indigenous inhabitants, it also created tension with authorities who sought to avoid such conflict. Pennsylvania's eighteenth-century politics were shaped in part by the struggle between migrants and their allies on the one hand, many of them Presbyterians with links to the Scottish Church, and the Quaker elite in the east, whose pacifist doctrine and commercial interests inclined them towards peace with their Indigenous neighbours.[1]

Those who remained in Philadelphia were more likely to be skilled craftsmen and labourers like Aitken, or else merchants, lawyers, and other professionals. Although it had competition from New York, Boston, and elsewhere, Philadelphia remained the leading commercial centre of mainland North America, trading with Britain's Caribbean colonies as well as with Scottish and English ports themselves. Local craft manufacturing had expanded during the Seven Years War, when transatlantic trade suffered disruption. In the war's aftermath, a larger community of artisans felt the pinch of renewed competition as well as the end of army purchases. These hard times, combined with the rising pitch of imperial crisis during the 1760s, were the origins of an increasingly militant working-class politics in the city. By the time Aitken arrived in 1773, Philadelphia's workers were more unified and confident than any in the colonies.[2]

This militant trajectory first became noticeable in 1765, when a crowd of city labourers tried to pull down Benjamin Franklin's house. Already nearly sixty years old, Franklin had long been considered a champion of ordinary Pennsylvanians: a former leather-aproned artisan himself, he had spent a decade opposing the colony's wealthy proprietors, Anglican descendants of the colony's founder William Penn. He was also an opponent of the Stamp Act, the ostensible cause of the riots in colonial port cities that summer. Yet Franklin was a leading advocate for making Pennsylvania a royal colony, as a means of wresting it from the proprietors' hands. What was more, he worked behind the scenes as the colony's agent in London to get an ally appointed stamp commissioner. Those facts were enough to make the absent Franklin's house a target for the

----

1 On the politics of frontier settlement and Quaker pacifism, see Kevin Kenny, *Peaceable Kingdom Lost: The Paxton Boys and the Destruction of William Penn's Holy Experiment* (Oxford University Press, 2011); Patrick Spero, *Frontier Country: The Politics of War in Early Pennsylvania* (University of Pennsylvania Press, 2016).

2 Gary Nash, *The Urban Crucible: The Northern Seaports and the Origins of the American Revolution* (Harvard University Press, 1979), p. 377.

outraged crowd, although his friends succeeded in preventing its destruction.[3]

Whether they were Quakers or not, the established merchants of Philadelphia proved more conservative in the years after 1763 than those of Boston or New York. The result was that such men failed to dominate the leadership of the emerging patriot movement. Instead, it was men like the former teacher Charles Thomson, brought up as an orphan in the family of a blacksmith, who stepped up to take the reins. Breaking from an alliance with Franklin in 1765, Thomson urged Philadelphia's reluctant commercial community to adopt the non-importation agreements that were being adopted elsewhere. 'So exasperated are the people', he noted that November, that merchants were obliged to act 'for their own safety'.[4]

Influence and intimidation were effective, but the city's working people also sought direct representation in the halls of power. In the summer of 1770, they formed a Patriotic Society intended to support electoral candidates. Taking inspiration from John Wilkes's supporters in London, these patriot mechanics declared their wish to 'preserve, inviolate, our just rights and privileges . . . against every attempt to violate or infringe the same, either here, or on the other side [of] the Atlantic'.[5] Writing in the *Pennsylvania Gazette*, one carpenter encouraged comrades to stand for election themselves. 'Let us step forth like men sensible of our true interest,' he counselled, 'and convince the great ones that truly wise and honest men, worthy to represent a free people, can be found amongst us.'[6] Joseph Parker, a tailor, was duly elected to the colonial assembly.

Genteel sceptics talked about Philadelphia's politicised working class

---

3 Ronald Schultz, *The Republic of Labor: Philadelphia Artisans and the Politics of Class, 1720–1830* (Oxford University Press, 1993), p. 31; and see Benjamin Newcomb, 'The Effect of the Stamp Act on Colonial Pennsylvania Politics', *William and Mary Quarterly* 23, no. 2 (April 1966), pp. 257–72.

4 Thomas Doerflinger, 'Philadelphia Merchants and the Logic of Moderation, 1760–1775', *William and Mary Quarterly* 40, no. 2 (April 1983), p. 218.

5 Charles Olton, 'Philadelphia's Mechanics in the First Decade of Revolution, 1765–1775', *Journal of American History* 59, no. 2 (September 1972), p. 323.

6 A Brother Chip, *Pennsylvania Gazette*, 27 September 1770, p. 3.

in much the same outraged tone as their counterparts in 1760s London. 'The poorest labourer upon the shore of the Delaware thinks himself entitled to deliver his sentiments in matters of religion or politics with as much freedom as the gentleman or scholar', as one Anglican clergyman put it in 1772.[7] That year, taking another leaf from the Wilkites' book, Philadelphia mechanics forced the colonial assembly to publish its debates and admit public observers. Meanwhile, the number of artisans elected to public office was growing. Merchants' political hegemony was waning.[8]

In London, Franklin was one of the few Americans who utterly rejected Wilkes's leadership of the imperial and parliamentary reform movements. His position in Pennsylvania politics makes that stance easier to understand. Franklin would not return to Philadelphia until May 1775, his path crossing with Aitken's voyage back to England. By then, a decade of working-class organising against recalcitrant merchants as well as ministerial tyranny had put down strong revolutionary foundations. In Philadelphia, more than in any other city of the empire, it was the labourers who led the way – and men like Franklin who had to catch up.

If there was one event that did most to precipitate a revolution in British America, it was what James Aitken called 'the riots at Boston', when a well-organised crowd – many disguised with coal-blackened faces and Mohawk Indian costumes – carried out an act of ritual destruction, 'sinking the tea, and insulting the friends of government'.[9] The event, later known as the Boston Tea Party, involved scores of the city's working

---

7 Gary Nash, *The Unknown American Revolution: The Unruly Birth of Democracy and the Struggle to Create America* (Penguin, 2005), p. 96.

8 For growing artisan power in the city, see also Charles Olton, *Artisans for Independence: Philadelphia Mechanics and the American Revolution* (Syracuse University Press, 1975); and Richard Alan Ryerson, *The Revolution Is Now Begun: The Radical Committees of Philadelphia, 1765–1776* (University of Pennsylvania Press, 1978).

9 [James Aitken,] *Life of James Aitken* (Winchester, 1777), p. 18.

men. Among them were the shoemaker George Hewes, who had once (like Aitken) hoped to join the British Army, and the blacksmith Joshua Wyeth, who remembered that the crowd was led by apprentices and journeymen like himself, 'living with tory masters'.[10] What happened that night in Boston was not just a strike against imperial authority. It was also an assertion of power from below.

Was Aitken himself there that December, dumping tea into the freezing harbour alongside Hewes and Wyeth? According to the life story published soon after his execution, he was. 'I cannot deny being very active in those riots', claimed the pamphlet, and as a result 'I did not escape the notice of many principal persons among the Americans'.[11] This claim, however, seems unlikely. It does not fit with the rest of Aitken's story, or the picture it paints of his journey through America. Most likely, his editor added it to help readers link Aitken's own acts of sabotage with the most famous case of revolutionary property destruction in the colonies. What is also likely is that Aitken did indeed take part in crowd action over the ill-fated tea – not in Boston, but 300 miles away in Philadelphia.

The story of the tea begins with the travails of the British East India Company, which had already done its part to cause the financial panic that swept through the empire in 1772. Because Company tea had to be taxed and auctioned off in London before it could be shipped westwards to the colonies, it faced stiff competition from so-called Dutch tea smuggled by local merchants. At the same time, tea was the only import still being taxed under the Townshend Acts of 1767, making it a highly contested symbol of imperial interference already. When, in the summer of 1773, Parliament chose to prop up the East India Company by allowing direct consignments to the colonies, a new showdown became inevitable.

George III's government in London, now under the leadership of

10 Alfred Young, *The Shoemaker and the Tea Party: Memory and the American Revolution* (Beacon Press, 1999), p. 43. The classic account of the affair is Benjamin Labaree, *The Boston Tea Party* (Oxford University Press, 1964); more recently see Benjamin Carp, *Rebels Rising: The Boston Tea Party and the Making of America* (Yale University Press, 2010).

11 [Aitken,] *Life*, p. 18.

Frederick North, had no idea what it was getting into. After all, the policy change promised to make tea cheaper as well as more plentiful in British North America – what could be the problem with that? But, after nearly ten years of resistance to imperial authority, colonists had built up certain attitudes towards Atlantic trade. The 1773 Tea Act was offensive because it treated them as mere tools in the government's effort to bail out the corrupt East India Company, because it reinforced the Company's monopoly on the tea trade, and because it looked like a ruse to dupe Americans into paying the Townshend duty. That, at least, was the case made with great effect by the seaport towns' patriot agitators.

A tide of outrage and popular mobilisation began to rise in October, as the details of the Tea Act became clear. In Philadelphia, a public meeting organised by Charles Thomson and others selected a delegation to pressure the merchants scheduled to receive and sell the tea. Only one of the two firms conceded fully to the patriots' demands. As the public clamour grew louder, the Edinburgh-trained surgeon Benjamin Rush wrote that the Company tea-chests contained 'a slow poison . . . the seeds of SLAVERY'.[12] Within another month, John Dickinson – perhaps the best-known lawyer in the city, as well as one of the wealthiest – joined his pen to the growing anti-tea campaign. His involvement showed the breadth of the movement in the city, even among moderates.

By December, the campaign had reached its highest pitch. Ominous notices signed by 'the committee for tarring and feathering' threatened any pilot who brought the tea-bearing ship *Polly* into harbour. As for her captain, they advised him to 'secure your ship against the rafts of combustible matter which may be set on fire and turned loose against her'.[13] An article by 'A Mechanic' summarised the depth of evil attributed to the 'detestable tea-scheme'. To understand where it was all heading, Philadelphians should look to India itself, where 'tyranny, plunder, oppression, and bloodshed' at the hands of the East India Company had

---

12 Hamden [Benjamin Rush], *Pennsylvania Journal*, 20 October 1773, quoted in Labaree, *Boston Tea Party*, p. 100.

13 Facsimile in Frederick Stone, 'How the Landing of Tea Was Opposed in Philadelphia by Colonel William Bradford and Others in 1773', *Pennsylvania Magazine of History and Biography* 15, no. 4 (1891), pp. 390–1.

reduced 'whole provinces [to] the distresses of oppression, slavery, famine, and the sword'.[14]

Finally, on Christmas Day, word reached Philadelphia that the *Polly* had appeared downriver at Chester. A committee of resistance leaders decided to meet the captain and escort him overland to the city, where he could get a true sense of the people's feelings. Two days later, as many as 8,000 citizens turned out to demonstrate their opposition to the tea – roughly a quarter of the population. If Aitken was directly involved in Americans' rejection of the tea, it would have been as part of this well-ordered crowd. The *Polly*'s captain got the message. He agreed to go back to the Delaware and turn his ship around.

All this could be accounted as a triumph for moderation, considering the broad base of resistance and the avoidance of any actual violence or property damage. In Philadelphia, mere threats had been enough. Yet tensions remained severe between the artisan community and the merchant elite. At the mass demonstration on 27 December, Charles Thomson called successfully on the assembled Philadelphians to endorse the Bostonians' 'spirited conduct in destroying their tea'.[15] Had the *Polly* made it to her wharf, the people effectively declared, they too would have done what Hewes, Wyeth, and their friends did. Much to the dismay of moderates like Dickinson, Philadelphia's working class kept faith with their comrades in Boston.

It took a ship a few weeks to cross the Atlantic in the eighteenth century – and winter months were worst for sailing. That meant it was some time before Americans began to find out how the British government would respond to their campaign against the East India Company tea. A newcomer in Philadelphia and a runaway to boot, James Aitken must have found those first few months precarious. But Philadelphia was big enough to always have some room for strangers. Houses and shops

---

14 A Mechanic, *Pennsylvania Gazette*, 8 December 1773, p. 3.

15 Mary Beth Norton, *1774: The Long Year of Revolution* (Vintage, 2021 [2020]), p. 36.

always needed painting, too, so men with Aitken's skills could generally pick up work. Somehow, anyway, he got through the winter. And, with the thaw, news started to trickle in from London.

Boston, it soon became clear, was to bear the brunt of the British government's fury over the tea. All the details did not reach the colonies until the summer, but the gist of the ministry's policy came sooner and was more than bad enough. The port of Boston was to be shut down entirely by Act of Parliament, flinging thousands of dockworkers, shipwrights, sailors, and associated tradesmen out of work, not to mention throwing local merchants' business and the regional economy into confusion. The port was to be reopened only if the town agreed to reimburse the East India Company for the lost tea, worth over £9,000 (£1.5 million today) – something Boston patriots would never countenance.

With the news of the port closure came General Thomas Gage, commander-in-chief of Britain's North American forces and now appointed governor of Massachusetts. As British ships prepared to blockade the harbour and regular soldiers arrived to bolster the city's garrison, Boston began to look like a city under siege. Further Acts of Parliament empowered Gage to dissolve the colonial assembly, restrict town meetings to once a year, and to quarter his troops in unoccupied buildings. They also provided that officials and soldiers could be tried overseas – rather than face a Massachusetts jury – if charged with offences while they carried out their duties. In short, all signs indicated a ministry fully prepared to crush colonial dissent with violence.

If Lord North and his cabinet thought they could confine the conflict to Massachusetts, though, they were mistaken. Even before the Boston silversmith Paul Revere rode into Philadelphia with news of the port closure, Philadelphians were debating how to support the resistance. For much of 1774, life in Philadelphia took place under the shadow of a sharpening imperial confrontation. Among the city's politicised workers, Aitken was soon drawn into speculation on the colonies' future. Having grown in self-confidence in the years since 1770, artisans and their supporters proved powerful advocates of solidarity with Boston and a robust, radical response to ministerial oppression.

On the day the port closure came into effect, Philadelphians marked the occasion with a 'solemn pause' – muffled church bells rang constantly, shops were shut, and citizens were encouraged to set their minds to the crisis of imperial governance.[16] As a public show of support for Bostonians, the event helped galvanise the city's patriots. But there were still conservatives, especially the Quaker merchants, who aimed to damp down the spirit of resistance. They refused to take part in the solemn pause. Then, when plans were made for a Continental Congress to be held in the city that September, they used their majority in the colonial assembly to appoint a slate of mostly conservative delegates. Their leader, the speaker of the assembly, was an old ally of Benjamin Franklin and the Quakers, Joseph Galloway.

Galloway was deeply suspicious of the extra-legal committees and mass meetings that had led opposition to the Tea Act and were now pushing for radical action – ideally a renewed boycott on British imports. He accused the patriots of 'setting up anarchy above order', and of instituting 'the beginning of republicanism'.[17] With the backing of Pennsylvania's delegation, Galloway hoped to use the Continental Congress to redirect the resistance movement. Rather than escalate the conflict, he wanted to renegotiate the basis of empire. Under his plan, the colonies would have their own legislative council, with power to veto Acts of Parliament affecting them. They would also remain firmly under imperial rule, with a 'President General' appointed by the king.

Would Galloway's plan have got anywhere with Lord North and George III? It seems unlikely, but he never had the chance to find out. As soon as the delegates arrived in Philadelphia that September, it became clear that the initiative lay with the more militant delegates, especially those from Virginia and Massachusetts. Their alliance with Philadelphia workers was cemented by two early decisions: first, to meet in Carpenter's Hall (rather than the State House, as Galloway suggested), and second, to appoint artisan leader Charles Thomson as Congress's secretary. In spite

---

16 Ryerson, *Revolution Is Now Begun*, pp. 43–4.

17 A Freeman [Joseph Galloway], 'To the Representatives of the Province', 21 July 1774, quoted in Ryerson, *Revolution Is Now Begun*, p. 61.

of support from New York's conservative delegation, Galloway's plan was voted down. Congress then turned its attention to planning an all-out economic struggle.

The plan Congress adopted in October, known as the Continental Association, bore many hallmarks of working-class influence. Not only did it institute a comprehensive, cross-colony non-importation agreement, but it also incorporated a vision of public virtue and moral economy. Gambling and extravagant entertainments were to be frowned upon. Merchants and manufacturers were forbidden from raising their prices to benefit from likely shortages. Most importantly, local committees were empowered to enforce the agreement and identify 'the enemies of American liberty'.[18] It was exactly the kind of thing Galloway had complained about a few months earlier – under duress, he signed off on the plan now, making it officially unanimous.

Congress's endorsement of local committees as the front line in the struggle against tyranny was a triumph for militant workers and their allies. Handing power to grass roots patriots, rather than hoarding it in distant provincial assemblies, helped to put ordinary people at the forefront of the movement. In Philadelphia that November, the mechanic-led slate crushed its merchant-led opposition in elections to the city's own new Committee of Observation and Inspection. Workers' resolve was bolstered by the knowledge that their counterparts elsewhere, in both the cities and the countryside, were organising too. Time was fast running out for anyone who hoped to remain neutral in the conflict with the ministry. When the boycott kicked in that December, every citizen's loyalty would begin to be tested.

Between 1770 and 1774, the political battle-lines in Philadelphia aligned increasingly with the divisions between rich and poor, merchant and mechanic. But, of course, as in London, neither the elite nor the working class was monolithic. Gradations of wealth and power separated master

---

18 Continental Association, 20 October 1774; Founders Online.

craftsmen from the journeymen and apprentices they employed. Certain trades were also more lucrative and prestigious than others: clockmakers and goldsmiths, for instance, were usually better off than blacksmiths and tailors. These were all artisans proper, as distinct from more casual labourers (who might sometimes be no less skilled – sailors, for example). Then there were the indentured servants and, at the foot of the city's social scale, more than 700 enslaved workers, some owned by artisans themselves.[19]

Cutting across or sometimes along the grain of occupational categories were the ethnic and religious differences for which Philadelphia was famous. In decades past, especially when Quakers were at the peak of their dominance, religious affiliation was more likely than class to define a citizen's political loyalty. By 1774, when these divisions had begun to fade a little, it was still vital for working-class leaders like Charles Thomson to reach out directly to different denominations. Mechanics also made sure the city's German population was represented on their committees. Organising workers' power in the city involved actively building coalitions across the old dividing lines – including with sympathetic shopkeepers, merchants, and professionals. Conflict with the government in London helped to drive that process in the 1770s.

When James Aitken arrived in Philadelphia, probably not long before the anti-tea protests got going, he added yet another complex piece to the city's occupational, ethnic, and religious mosaic. As a Scotsman and a Presbyterian, he fit a reasonably familiar mould, and as a journeyman with craft skills he had a route into the mechanics' community. On the other hand, he was also an escaped indentured servant – a runaway, who might have someone on his trail. It was very likely he had robbed and stolen his way out of Virginia. From a certain perspective, Aitken was no more than one of the 'thieves, pick-pockets, low cheats and dirty sots'

19 On the internal distinctions and jealousies among Philadelphia artisans, see Eric Foner, *Tom Paine and Revolutionary America* (Oxford University Press, 1976), pp. 19–69; for the complex politics of the urban working class more generally, see Alfred Young, *Liberty Tree: Ordinary People and the American Revolution* (New York University Press, 2006), pp. 57–176.

that sober, upright artisans complained about, or one of the vagrants who ended up in the House of Betterment.[20]

Aitken was certainly in more fortunate circumstances than another recent arrival, Dinah Nevil. A twenty-nine-year-old woman of colour, Nevil had been working for a family in New Jersey when, in 1773, she and her four children were sold to a slave trader from Virginia. But Nevil did not accept the claim that she was a slave, or the idea that she and her family could be sold. When she arrived in Philadelphia that winter, for delivery to her new legal owner, Nevil appealed to the city's nascent anti-slavery movement for help. She was taken out of the slave trader's custody and placed in an almshouse, where conditions were so dire that two of her children died. There she stayed throughout 1774, while Philadelphians wrangled over the rights and wrongs of her situation, and indeed of slavery itself.[21]

It was probably Thomas Harrison, a tailor and constable who helped keep order in the city's Middle Ward, who first intervened to help Nevil and her children. The case bore a striking similarity to that of James Somerset in London a year earlier, which had, in turn, encouraged enslaved people in America to seek their freedom. Like Somerset's, though, Nevil's case rested on a legal technicality – because she claimed Indigenous ancestry, she was protected by a Pennsylvania law that forbade the enslavement of Native Americans. Like Somerset's too, Nevil's case was backed by high-profile anti-slavery campaigners, men like Benjamin Rush and Anthony Benezet, who could mobilise legal resources on her behalf. Even so, Nevil never actually won her freedom in court. In 1779, Harrison helped scrape together the money to buy it instead.

Nearer the other end of the scale of new arrivals in the city was Thomas Paine. At thirty-seven, Paine was a master craftsman, having

---

20 'Wilbraham', *Pennsylvania Packet*, 24 March 1781, quoted in Foner, *Tom Paine*, p. 52.

21 For Nevil's story and its complexities for historians, see Kirsten Sword, 'Remembering Dinah Nevil: Strategic Deceptions in Eighteenth-Century Antislavery', *Journal of American History* 97, no. 2 (September 2010), pp. 315–43; see also Gary Nash, *Forging Freedom: The Formation of Philadelphia's Black Community, 1720–1840* (Harvard University Press, 1988), p. 43.

learned from his father the art of making stays for women's clothes. He had also been a customs officer and a tobacconist, moving around the south-east of England. His skill with a pen helped bring him to the attention of Benjamin Franklin in London – and Franklin's recommendation went a long way in Philadelphia. Paine had suffered his share of misfortune, too. His first wife died in pregnancy, he lost his business and his customs post, and separated from his second wife. He was so ill when he arrived in Philadelphia, in November 1774, that he had to be carried from the ship.[22]

Paine and Aitken scarcely overlapped in Philadelphia, but they had been in the same place at the same time a year before – in London, 1773, when Paine took part in a campaign for better pay for customs officers like himself. The older man's activities and inclinations likely made him a far more perceptive observer than Aitken of labour struggle and dissident politics in the metropolis. He was already acquainted with the work of thinkers such as Joseph Priestley and Catherine Macaulay, whose critiques of British government gave intellectual depth to the Wilkite opposition movement. Within a year of reaching Philadelphia, Paine was already at work on his polemical masterpiece, *Common Sense*. 'Every spot of the old world is overrun with oppression', it declared. 'The cause of America is in a great measure the cause of all mankind.'[23]

Three migrants to Philadelphia on the eve of the American Revolution – Aitken, Nevil, and Paine – represent some of the vast diversity of Britain's imperial and Atlantic working class. For all their enormous differences, they also shared experiences – poverty, weakness, injustice, and yet hope as well – that helped their visions of the world to overlap, at least a little. Another migrant who had been in London in the summer of 1773 was the African-born poet Phillis Wheatley, then still held in

---

22 In addition to Foner, *Tom Paine*, see Mark Philp, *Paine* (Oxford University Press, 1989); John Keane, *Tom Paine: A Political Life* (Bloomsbury, 1996); Harvey Kaye, *Thomas Paine: Firebrand of the Revolution* (Oxford University Press, 2000); and for a provocative account of Paine's thought, J.C.D. Clark, *Thomas Paine: Britain, America, and France in the Age of Enlightenment and Revolution* (Oxford University Press, 2018).

23 Anon. [Thomas Paine], *Common Sense* (Philadelphia, 1776).

slavery. The next year, back in Boston and manumitted by her former owners, Wheatley wrote to the Mohegan Presbyterian minister Samson Occum. 'In every human breast', she wrote, there is 'a principle, which we call love of freedom'.[24] That was something workers of all races knew better than their rulers.

From December 1774, with the explicit backing of the Continental Congress, local patriot committees took up the role of enforcing the boycott on imports from Britain. In fact, the restrictions extended further than that, for commodities like tea were highly discouraged – and from the spring of 1775, banned – regardless of their origin. Patriot gentlemen took to wearing homespun woollen cloth instead of fine, imported fabric – diminishing, as a side effect, the visible distinction between rich and poor. Merchants and consumers who flouted the boycott were threatened with humiliation and violence, 'delivered over', as the conservative New Yorker Samuel Seabury put it, 'to the vengeance of a lawless, outrageous mob'.[25] Those who expected deference from ordinary people found the balance of day-to-day power shifting beneath their feet.

James Aitken, at this moment, might have embraced the patriot cause as Thomas Paine did. Mobilising his identity and skills as a journeyman painter, he could have remained in Philadelphia and built a life there. When Philadelphians formed volunteer militia associations the following spring, Aitken could finally have become a soldier – even, in time, an officer, as he had so long dreamed. But, once again, the path of solidarity

24 Phillis Wheatley to Samson Occum, printed in *Connecticut Gazette*, 11 March 1774; see David Waldstreicher, 'Ancients, Moderns, and Africans: Phillis Wheatley and the Politics of Empire and Slavery in the American Revolution', *Journal of the Early Republic* 37, no. 4 (Winter 2017), pp. 701–33, pp. 701–2. For Wheatley's life see Vincent Caretta, *Phillis Wheatley Peters: Biography of a Genius in Bondage* (University of Georgia Press, 2011); and David Waldstreicher, *The Odyssey of Phillis Wheatley: A Poet's Journeys Through American Slavery and Independence* (Farrar, Straus and Giroux, 2023).

25 A Farmer [Samuel Seabury], *Free Thoughts on the Proceedings of the Continental Congress . . .* (New York, 1775), pp. 35–6.

with fellow workers was not the one Aitken took. He was still only twenty-one years old.

It may have been that Aitken's first encounter with the Committee of Observation and Inspection saw him on the wrong side of the new dispensation. Gambling was sternly frowned upon in the Association signed by Congress, and Aitken could easily have found himself part of a game disrupted by zealous committeemen. The lifestyle he had favoured back in London was a long way from the pious, strait-laced virtues envisioned by some dissident writers and activists. Samuel Adams, a leader of the Boston Sons of Liberty, hoped to create a Christian Sparta. That was hardly Aitken's idea of a good time. Aitken was also something of a young contrarian. When Philadelphians spoke of their campaign against British tyranny, he had the chutzpah to pipe up with the opposing arguments. It was not a strategy calculated to win friends and influence his fellow artisans.

However exactly it came about, Aitken left Philadelphia early in 1775. His next destination, Perth Amboy, was a New Jersey port town situated at the mouth of the Raritan River, just opposite the southern tip of Staten Island. It lay some seventy miles east of Philadelphia, a walk of two or three days. What was interesting about Perth Amboy from Aitken's perspective, though, was its Scottish connection – the town had been founded by Scots in the seventeenth century and had continued to receive migrants from Scotland in disproportionate numbers.[26] It was also, at the outbreak of the American Revolution, a bastion of loyalty to the British Empire. Perhaps someone in Philadelphia told Aitken it would suit him there. If so, they probably meant it as an insult.

Perth Amboy was, of course, an even smaller town than Philadelphia. As the economic slowdown caused by the trade boycott started to bite, work for a newcomer like Aitken was inevitably scarce. By spring, in any case, he seems to have decided that his sojourn in the colonies had gone on long enough. His intention had only ever been to escape the authorities in London after his spate of highway robbery and housebreaking. After a

26 On Perth Amboy and its Scottish connection, see Ned Landsman, *Scotland and Its First American Colony, 1683–1765* (Princeton University Press, 1985).

year away, the constables in the metropolis had surely forgotten all about him – but he hoped his friends had not. Returning to London, he was keen to resume the life of debauchery and petty criminality he had begun there. He was not interested in being part of any grand political experiment.

Making his way back to London was not an altogether simple task for someone with no money or connections. But Aitken was nothing if not an intrepid traveller. He had already crossed the Middle Colonies as an escapee from bondage in Virginia. This time, there would be no indenture – there was no shortage of labour in the British Isles, after all. There was, however, a shortage of hands willing to work ships travelling eastwards across the Atlantic. Too many men made only the westbound journey, in search of a better life in North America. From Perth Amboy Aitken went first to New York, then he sailed coastwise south to North Carolina (perhaps Wilmington) where he finally managed to negotiate a place on board an ocean-going ship.

The only problem was that Aitken's ship was bound for Liverpool, not London. He would have to make the rest of the trip overland. Meanwhile, on the voyage home, Aitken might have had one more chance to contemplate the nature of the British Empire – for if there was one thing Liverpool shipping was famous for, it was participation in the Atlantic slave trade. At least one ship from the city, the *Two Brothers*, left the southern mainland of North America on a homeward voyage in the spring of 1775. She had brought enslaved people from the Gambia for sale in Savannah, Georgia, and points north. Twenty of her crew died on the way west from Africa – and so did sixty-five (or nearly one in every five) of the men, women, and children she had dragged across the sea in chains.[27]

---

27 Details from the Trans-Atlantic Slave Trade Database, slavevoyages.org.

PART II

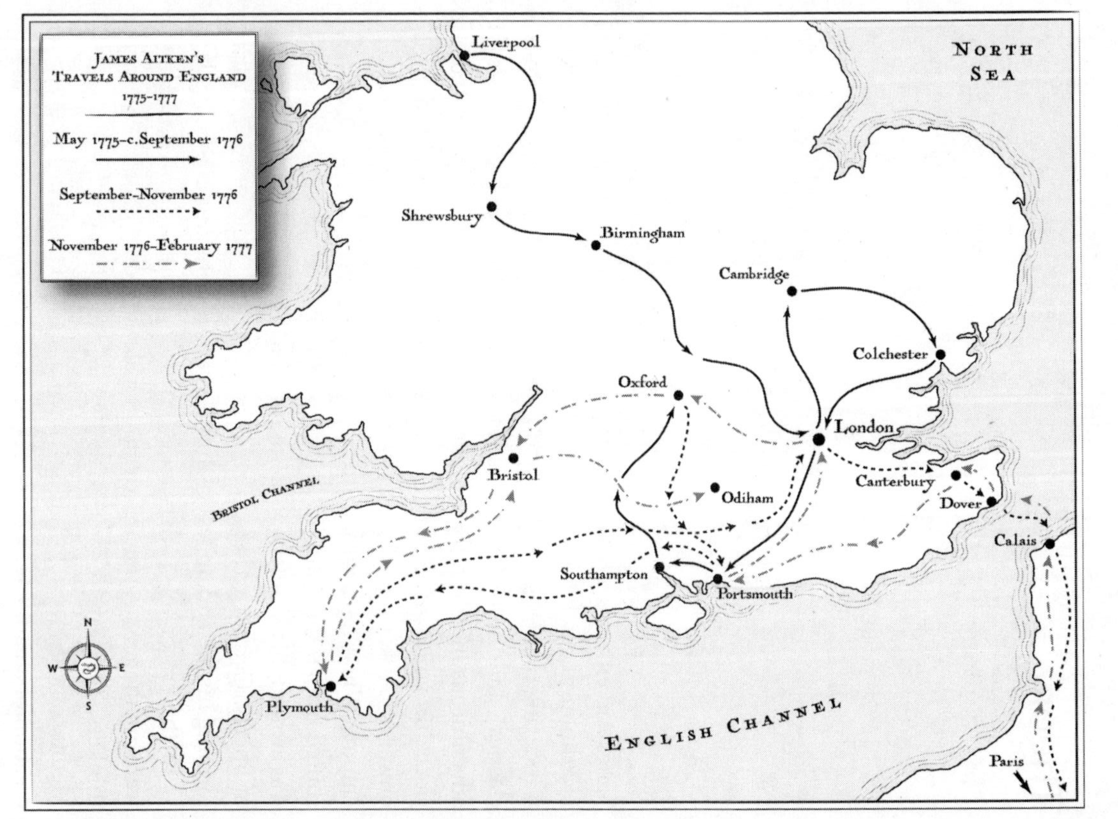

North Sea
Liverpool
Shrewsbury
Birmingham
Cambridge
Colchester
London
Oxford
Bristol
Bristol Channel
Odiham
Southampton
Portsmouth
Canterbury
Dover
Calais
Paris
Plymouth
English Channel
James Aitken's 'Travels Around England' 1775–1777
May 1775–c.September 1776
September–November 1776
November 1776–February 1777
N
E
S
W

5

Theory

James Aitken was a reader. He acquired a taste for books as a schoolboy in Edinburgh, and it did not abandon him during the years of work and wandering that followed. He read translations of the Greek and Roman classics, and more recent authors like Voltaire. He read tales of adventurous men and their desperate deeds, which had captivated him since his youth. And, of course, he read about politics. From 1774 onwards, Aitken's world was overshadowed by the crisis of Britain's empire. When he returned from the colonies in 1775, his engagement shifted from immediate events towards the world of words and theory. It was around this moment, it seems, that he became transfixed by the idea of liberty. Certain writers, certain notions, took hold of Aitken, transforming his life and, in less than two years, leading him to his death.

In the era of the American Revolution, British theorists of liberty were building on a long and rich political tradition. Like other European thinkers, they could look back to the civil struggles of the ancient Mediterranean world. The subversion of the Roman republic and creation of an autocratic empire, resisted by heroic figures such as Cato (who fought Caesar) and Brutus (who killed him), were at the heart of many people's ideas about the workings of political freedom. In Britain, though, the seventeenth century's civil wars had prompted a new outpouring of political thought – in defence of the state's power, as in Thomas Hobbes's *Leviathan*, but also in opposition to monarchical tyranny. The struggles for religious and political power between 1639 and 1689 created space for radical experiments, like the Diggers' short-lived attempts at common ownership, and for ideas about a common-wealth of citizens rooted in natural equality.[1]

England's republic may have been overthrown in 1660, when Charles II was placed on the throne of his executed father, but the political ideas of that era were never completely rooted out. Less than a generation later, Charles's younger brother James II was chased from the throne in favour of his niece Mary and her Dutch husband, William of Orange. The 1688 coup, backed up by a bloody military campaign against James's supporters in Ireland, helped to establish the English state as a collaboration between Crown and Parliament – and vindicated the doctrine of legitimate revolution against tyranny developed by John Locke a decade earlier. It also, as importantly, confirmed Protestant supremacy and the suppression of Catholicism throughout the new monarchs' dominions. For its supporters, known as the Whigs, 1688 was the Glorious Revolution. In the form of a constitutional monarchy, the state it created was both powerful and, from their perspective, free.[2]

By the 1740s, the heirs of the Whig triumph in 1688 faced two kinds of political threat. One, from the Jacobite sympathisers of the deposed Stuart dynasty, was decisively defeated in 1746. The other, however, would prove more difficult to pin down – this was the revival of the commonwealth tradition. Commonwealthmen were no Jacobites, and

1 For a recent account of this tradition, see Quentin Skinner, *Liberty as Independence: The Making and Unmaking of a Political Ideal* (Cambridge University Press, 2025); and, more broadly, Annelien de Dijn, *Freedom: An Unruly History* (Harvard University Press, 2020). A popular tradition of liberty is traced from the English Revolution to the end of the eighteenth century in Peter Linebaugh and Marcus Rediker, *The Many-Headed Hydra: Sailors, Slaves, Commoners and the Hidden History of the Revolutionary Atlantic* (Verso, 2000).

2 See Kathleen Wilson, 'Inventing Revolution: 1688 and Eighteenth-Century Popular Politics', *Journal of British Studies* 28, no. 4 (October 1989), pp. 349–86; Steven Pincus, *1688: The First Modern Revolution* (Yale University Press, 2009).

nor were they really opponents of monarchy itself. But they placed a far higher premium on liberty than on state power. From this perspective, the Whigs in government had betrayed their commitment to the natural rights and equality of citizens by strengthening the hand of the executive, using bribes to stifle parliamentary opposition. As its empire and commerce grew, Britain was sinking into corruption, its politics increasingly captive to the degrading and centralising pull of money.[3]

Such an attitude appealed to country gentlemen and even noblemen who found themselves disconnected and out of favour – and who resented government expenditure that inevitably meant taxes. In this sense, commonwealth thought was a distinctly elite and conservative phenomenon. It even attracted former Jacobites and Tories, the Whigs' inveterate opponents.[4] What commonwealthmen of this type most wanted was to be left alone so they could enjoy their enormous privilege in peace, without needing to contribute to the expenses of imperial war or compete for status with men newly enriched by gains from commerce or finance. They saw conspiracies everywhere and feared all power that was not their own. It was an attractive ideology not only to disgruntled British aristocrats, but also to plenty of American slave owners.

Yet these were not the only kinds of people drawn to the common-wealth tradition. Central to the emerging coalition by the middle of the eighteenth century were Protestant dissenters – those who belonged to churches outside the established Church of England and, as a result, suffered an array of disadvantages and official exclusions. Dissenters could not attend the two great universities at Oxford and Cambridge, nor could they be officers in the armed forces or Members of Parliament.

---

3 See Caroline Robbins, *Eighteenth-Century Commonwealthmen: Studies in the Transmission, Development and Circumstances of English Liberal Thought from the Restoration of Charles II Until the War with the Thirteen Colonies* (Harvard University Press, 1959); Bernard Bailyn, *The Ideological Origins of the American Revolution* (Harvard University Press, 1967).

4 Links between opposition Whig and Tory thought were forged, in particular, by Viscount Bolingbroke in the 1720s and '30s: see Isaac Kramnick, *Bolingbroke and His Circle: The Politics of Nostalgia in the Age of Walpole* (Cornell University Press, 1992); David Armitage, 'A Patriot for Whom? The Afterlives of Bolingbroke's Patriot King', *Journal of British Studies* 36, no. 4 (October 1997), pp. 397–418.

While these things were all rather distant for most people, that made the exclusion all the more galling for those whose wealth and status would have otherwise granted them entry. For dissenters, religious exclusion was a form of oppression that could be readily traced back to an overmighty state and a corrupt, self-interested elite.[5]

In the American colonies, dissenting Protestant religion was deeprooted and widespread. Colonists easily, if a little disingenuously, traced the origins of their settlements to true believers fleeing religious persecution during the struggles of the seventeenth century. Across the Atlantic, moreover, it was hard to see politics in London as anything other than distant, corrupt, and deeply unrepresentative. The commonwealth tradition therefore found a receptive audience. By the 1760s, it had come to deeply shape American political consciousness. On top of everything else, it provided a political language that could bridge the gap between the plantation establishment of the south and the Puritan-inflected civic culture of the north. When British colonial policy began to change at the close of the Seven Years War, it was all too easy for Americans to diagnose corruption and conspiracy. That was exactly what their philosophy predicted.

There was more than a hint of this commonwealth lineage in the political worlds that James Aitken had already encountered by 1775 – in the Presbyterian populists of the Church of Scotland, among the supporters of John Wilkes in London, and in the rhetoric of well-read Pennsylvanians like Charles Thomson and John Dickinson. Before he arrived back in England that spring, though, Aitken had not yet been confronted with a version of that kind of thought that spoke directly and coherently to men like him. Or if he had, he had been in no mood to hear it. As the crisis intensified on both sides of the ocean after 1774, British writers sharpened their critiques of the government. Their theories soon

---

5 On the Protestant dissenting tradition and its contribution to the politics of liberty, see E.P. Thompson, *The Making of the English Working Class* (Penguin, 2013 [1963]), pp. 28–58; J.C.D. Clark, *English Society 1688–1832* (Cambridge University Press, 1985), pp. 277–9; James E. Bradley, *Religion, Revolution, and English Radicalism: Non-Conformity in Eighteenth-Century Politics and Society* (Cambridge University Press, 2002).

cut to the foundations of Britain's empire, assaulting the state in the name of freedom. Soon enough, even Aitken was listening.

England, as James Aitken found it in 1775, was already a different country from the one he had escaped two years before. Now twenty-two years old, Aitken arrived in Liverpool in May and made his way slowly south over much of the rest of the year. His path took him through Birmingham and Coventry, towns already transforming and rapidly growing as the early Industrial Revolution took hold, as well as through market towns and country villages. Aitken occasionally robbed a roadside shop to pay his way, but he also found a new source of income – enlisting, for a bonus, in the army regiments being raised for the expected American war. Having already learned the art of slipping away from unwanted authorities, it was easy enough for Aitken to pocket the king's shilling and run.

War on the horizon helped focus British minds. For many, that meant no further contemplation of the rights or wrongs of empire. After shots were fired in the Massachusetts villages of Lexington and Concord in April, and George III declared the colonies to be in a state of rebellion that August, there were plenty of his subjects who considered the American cause now beyond the pale. Loyalty to Britain and its empire was paramount, above more theoretical political considerations. Many others, though, responded differently. War with the colonies was a disaster that they still hoped to avert. Yet, the more the government appeared committed to the violent suppression of the colonists, the more it simply proved the point that Britain's empire was built on tyranny. For those concerned with liberty, it was increasingly clear something had to change.[6]

---

6 On the intellectual and cultural foundations of the pro-government response to the war, see Eliga Gould, *The Persistence of Empire: British Political Culture in the Age of the American Revolution* (University of North Carolina Press, 2000). For a sophisticated assessment of public opinion, see James E. Bradley, 'The British Public and the American Revolution: Ideology, Interest and Opinion', in H.T. Dickinson, ed., *Britain and the American Revolution* (Addison Wesley Longman, 1998), pp. 124–54, which draws on the earlier findings in Bradley, *Popular Politics and the American Revolution in England: Petitions, the Crown, and Public Opinion* (Mercer University Press, 1986).

Calls for American independence had in fact begun a full year earlier, in 1774, as Parliament considered its response to the destruction of the tea at Boston harbour. Josiah Tucker, no friend of the American cause in principle, nonetheless argued that independence was not only possible but also desirable from a British perspective. The military effort required to crush a rebellion there would simply be too great, Tucker predicted, and the economic impact of independence would be minimal. Just as Adam Smith would later suggest, Tucker thought commerce might actually improve once the restrictive regulations of empire were dismantled.[7]

Tucker's assessment pleased neither the government nor the colonists' friends, but it did open the door to new perspectives on the structure of the empire. In a series of letters to a London newspaper, Major John Cartwright – a well-connected former navy officer who had fought in the Seven Years War – set out a far more positive version of the proposal. Collected in a pamphlet titled *American Independence, the Interest and Glory of Great Britain*, Cartwright's letters argued that the colonies were 'sister kingdoms' in a larger British family. Anyone with 'common sense and common honesty' could see that Parliament had no right to rule peoples who were not (and could not practically be) represented in it. 'The most perfect freedom in America', he concluded, was the best route to 'the prosperity of Great Britain'.[8]

Another English advocate of radical imperial reform was Granville Sharp, the lawyer and activist who had led the campaign to free James Somerset from slavery in 1772. Sharp's pamphlet on empire, published soon after Cartwright's, focused more on Ireland than it did on the American colonies – but, in drawing the analogy between them, it made even clearer that British and English abuse of power went back to the

---

7 Josiah Tucker, *The True Interest of Britain* (London, 1774). See Salim Rashid, ' "He Startled . . . As If He Saw a Spectre": Tucker's Proposal for American Independence', *Journal of the History of Ideas* 43, no. 3 (September 1982), pp. 439–60.

8 John Cartwright, *American Independence, the Interest and Glory of Great Britain* (London, 1774), pp. 13, 3, 36. See Robert E. Toohey, *Liberty and Empire: British Radical Solutions to the American Problem, 1774–1776* (University of Kentucky Press, 1978), pp. 47–61.

medieval dawn of empire. Sharp drew on seventeenth-century theories of natural and international law to argue that one people could not legitimately rule another without including them in government. 'The people', as the title of his work declared, possessed 'a natural right to a share in the legislature'. 'All British subjects', including the Irish and Americans, were 'equally free by the law of nature'.[9]

Such thinkers did not retreat from their position in 1775. Cartwright's pamphlet was reissued in an expanded edition, and the caustic anti-ministerial newspaper *The Crisis* began its nearly two-year weekly run. Meanwhile Catherine Macaulay, a celebrated historian of seventeenth-century England whose brother was a close ally of John Wilkes, joined in with a polemic of her own. Writing directly 'to the people', Macaulay claimed that the government had 'attempted to wrest from our American colonists every privilege necessary to freemen'. She also paid particular attention to the recent Quebec Act, which recognised the Catholic establishment of Canada's French settler population – a concession to 'the Popish religion' that was, she wrote, 'altogether incompatible with the fundamental principles of our constitution'. War in America, she predicted, would mean the destruction of British prosperity and power.[10]

As Aitken wound his way south towards London that year, then, he had plenty of opportunity to engage with the notion that freedom and independence for the colonies would also be the best possible outcome for his own country. That was not something he had encountered in Philadelphia, or elsewhere in the colonies, the year before. At the same

---

9 Granville Sharp, *A Declaration of the People's Natural Right to a Share in the Legislature* (London, 1774), p. 2; Toohey, *Liberty and Empire*, pp. 62–71.

10 Catherine Macaulay, *An Address to the People of England, Scotland, and Ireland, on the Present Important Crisis of Affairs* (London, 1775), pp. 5, 7, 15; Toohey, *Liberty and Empire*, pp. 88–96. See also Lucy Martin Donnelly, 'The Celebrated Mrs Macaulay', *William and Mary Quarterly* 6, no. 2 (April 1949), pp. 173–207; Karen Green, *Catherine Macaulay's Republican Enlightenment* (Routledge, 2020); Max Skjonsberg, ed., *Catherine Macaulay: Political Writings* (Cambridge University Press, 2023). Mary Bilder has traced Macaulay's influence on the Declaration of Independence in a forthcoming essay in Tom Cutterham and Sara Georgini, eds, *Americans in Revolution: New Intellectual Histories* (University of Virginia Press, forthcoming).

time, these arguments were increasingly intermingled with a deeper critique of the British state. By 1775, the crisis of empire had given rise to a domestic political challenge. While the army and the government prepared for war, there were some British radicals who sought to lay the groundwork for what the authors of *The Crisis* called 'another revolution'.[11]

James Burgh was born and raised in Scotland, the son of a Church of Scotland minister. He was already in his late twenties when, after a brief stint as a linen-merchant, he came south to London, dabbled in printing, and at last became a teacher – the profession he would follow for the next twenty-five years, through the middle of the eighteenth century. Burgh ran a private academy in Newington Green, a village in the London suburbs, which catered to the children of Protestant dissenters. He also wrote books on education, religious toleration, and 'the dignity of human nature'. Nothing about this life dictated that Burgh would develop revolutionary politics. But in 1774, at the age of sixty, he began to publish the most dangerous book the British establishment had seen in a generation.[12]

Burgh's *Political Disquisitions*, subtitled 'an enquiry into public errors, defects, and abuses', spanned three volumes and might have been longer had its author lived to see the project through. It was at once a vast catalogue of historical anecdote, a digest of classical republican and

---

11 Neil York, 'George III, Tyrant: *The Crisis* as Critic of Empire, 1775–1776', *History* 94, no. 4 (October 2009), p. 445. See Neil York, ed., *The Crisis: A British Defense of the American Revolution, 1775–1776* (Liberty Fund, 2016), which contains the paper's complete run.

12 Burgh's only modern biography is Carla Hay, *James Burgh: Spokesman for Reform in Hanoverian England* (University Press of America, 1979). His influence in the American colonies is discussed in Oscar Handlin and Mary Handlin, 'James Burgh and American Revolutionary Theory', *Proceedings of the Massachusetts Historical Society* 73 (1961), pp. 38–57. For a critical response to this earlier scholarship, which tended to emphasise Burgh's moderation, see Isaac Kramnick, 'Republicanism Revisited: The Case of James Burgh', *Proceedings of the American Antiquarian Society* 102, no. 1 (April 1992), pp. 81–98.

modern commonwealth philosophy, and a sustained, acerbic criticism of the state of British politics. At the book's heart was an argument that 'all lawful authority . . . originates from the *people*' – and that Britain's existing political arrangements were far removed from any that might put such popular sovereignty into practice.[13] Burgh called for a democratic reconstruction of the British constitution, one that would root out established elites and restore power to ordinary citizens. What was more, he argued that if such reforms could not be implemented by the men in power, it would fall to the people to bring them about.

That was a process already underway in America. For writers like John Cartwright, Granville Sharp, Catherine Macaulay, and Burgh, events there sent a warning message to the British state – and a wake-up call to the British people. 'Rouse, my countrymen!' wrote Macaulay in the conclusion of her 1775 *Address*. 'Rouse! and unite in one general effort.'[14] Ostensibly, her call was for petitions to the king and Parliament. Those who could see through this shield from prosecution, though, might form a more radical interpretation.

It was not the British monarchy but Parliament that bore the brunt of this new wave of democratic critique. Since the days of the Stamp Act and Declaratory Act in the mid-1760s, American colonists had identified Parliament as their chief oppressor. Proposed solutions to the crisis – whether from Cartwright in England or from Joseph Galloway in Pennsylvania – focused on curbing parliamentary authority without removing royal sovereignty: the colonies were to be 'sister kingdoms', not strictly republics. The crucial point was that Americans were to be represented in their own elected legislatures, which would share power with the monarch under the same kind of constitutional limits that had been fixed for England in 1688. Yet the debate over representation for Americans soon bled into domestic politics, for the truth was that Parliament scarcely represented ordinary British people either.

'We know full well,' wrote Burgh, 'that it is but a very small part of the people of England whose votes fill the house of representatives.' The poor

---

13 James Burgh, *Political Disquisitions*, 3 vols (London, 1774–5), vol. 1, p. 3.
14 Macaulay, *Address to the People of England*, p. 29.

had just as much right to determine their own rulers as the rich, he argued, yet they were 'utterly deprived' of that power by restrictions on the franchise. At the same time, growing cities like Birmingham, Manchester, and Liverpool went almost without representation, while pocket boroughs in the countryside could send men to Parliament on a handful of votes. Both the restricted franchise and the absurdly unequal size of constituencies meant Parliament had no claim to true representation. That, in turn, made the British *an enslaved people*, a nation without liberty.[15]

On top of the skewed electoral system, democrats had identified several other serious 'errors, defects, and abuses' in Parliament. Long terms between elections, fixed at seven years since early in the eighteenth century, meant that its members all too easily ignored the voters' wishes. Instead, they often fell prey to 'bribery, corruption, and many other wicked arts' – pensions, jobs, or other favours were traded by government to secure the votes they needed for their schemes, regardless of the people's interests.[16] Whigs like Edmund Burke argued that MPs had to follow their own judgement.[17] In reality, without the check of regular and fair elections, many were simply bought and paid for. That was how a ruling class, and not the people, managed to rule Britain.

Burgh was not alone in pointing all this out. Cartwright, too, wrote that the corruption and inequality of parliamentary representation were 'in direct violation of the rights and interests of the nation collectively'.[18] John Wilkes and his friends had been drawing attention to the corrupt and self-serving parliamentary oligarchy since the 1760s. But, combined with events in the colonies, the election of 1774 gave renewed impetus to the critique. Although Wilkes himself was elected, the outcome disappointed the critics of government. Lord North, prime minister since 1770, emerged

---

15 Burgh, *Political Disquisitions*, vol. 1, pp. 25, 27, 37.

16 Ibid., p. 267.

17 See Lucy Sutherland, 'Edmund Burke and the Relations Between Members of Parliament and Their Constituents', *Studies in Burke and His Time* 10, no. 1 (Fall 1968), pp. 1005–21; Richard Bourke, *Empire and Revolution: The Political Life of Edmund Burke* (Princeton University Press, 2015), pp. 376–90.

18 Cartwright, *American Independence*, p. 42.

with increased support in the House of Commons – a result that only strengthened Burgh and others' conviction that Parliament itself was an instrument of oligarchy, not popular sovereignty.

'People in power had better avoid driving things to such an extremity, as to render their destruction necessary, or seemingly so', Burgh declared towards the end of his third and final volume. 'When the people take redress into their own hands, woe to the tyrants.'[19] He took inspiration not just from the classical and commonwealth authorities he cited, but from the American Congress and insurrectionary committees too. It was not '*particular* grievances' that had to be redressed. Rather, the country had to be restored to freedom. 'Instructing, petitioning, remonstrating, and the like' could never be effective means to such an end. Burgh left no doubt that it was revolution he envisaged. 'Let thy thunders shake the mountains', he asked God on the book's final page. 'Let the cause of civil and religious liberty prove victorious.'[20]

Having made his way south through England from Liverpool, James Aitken reached London before the end of 1775. There, he found a city in uproar over the government's plans for war in America. With John Wilkes's sponsorship as Lord Mayor, the freemen of the city had delivered repeated petitions to Parliament and George III, pleading against the policy of violent suppression. Merchants complained that war would ruin trade and lead to economic hardship. Wilkes himself declared it would be 'bloody, expensive, and a threat to liberty'. The government, he claimed, planned to 'establish despotism in New England, and popery in Canada'.[21] While Londoners opposing Wilkes flocked to sign loyal addresses to the king that autumn, the freemen nonetheless elected his ally John Sawbridge, Catherine Macaulay's brother, to succeed him as Lord Mayor. There was no escaping the din of political argument.

---

19 Burgh, *Political Disquisitions*, vol. 3, p. 446.

20 Ibid., pp. 455, 460.

21 Peter D.G. Thomas, *John Wilkes: A Friend to Liberty* (Oxford University Press, 1996), p. 169.

A little outside the metropolis, however, in the quiet and orderly village of Newington Green, it was possible to take a more considered, philosophical view of the crisis. Richard Price, the Welsh-born polymath and minister of the village's dissenting Unitarian church, was kept abreast of events in America by his network of friends on both sides of the ocean. Among them had been James Burgh, a Newington Green neighbour for decades, whose revolutionary politics was forged in conversation with Price and fellow dissenters. Benjamin Franklin, now serving in the Second Continental Congress in Philadelphia, was in touch with Price through fellow scientist and dissenting visionary Joseph Priestley. The milieu was rather intellectual compared with that of the average London coffee-house or pub. But Price's earnestness and commitment to principle led him, like Burgh, towards a radical set of political conclusions.[22]

What Price wrote that winter, and published in the new year, was a book of a little over 150 pages that set out, with startling clarity, a philosophy of liberty as it related both to the Americans and to his countrymen at home. 'An important revolution in the affairs of this kingdom seems to be approaching', Price concluded, that would present 'an opportunity (never perhaps to be recovered, if lost)' to root out all corruption and restore the constitution to a state of liberty. The outcome of the present crisis mattered as much to '*this country*' as it did to the colonies, whose independence in some form now seemed inevitable.[23] It was up to the British people, he implied, to take the necessary action.

Like his friend Burgh and his fellow democrats, Price rooted his politics in the principle of popular sovereignty. It was with the people, he insisted, that 'all legislative authority originates . . . Theirs is the only real omnipotence.'[24] In stating this case, he attacked the Whig doctrine of

22 Biographies of Price include Carl Cone, *Torchbearer of Freedom: The Influence of Richard Price on Eighteenth Century Thought* (University Press of Kentucky, 1952); D.O. Thomas, *The Honest Mind: The Thought and Work of Richard Price* (Oxford University Press, 1977); and Paul Frame, *Liberty's Apostle: Richard Price, His Life and Times* (University of Wales Press, 2015).

23 Richard Price, *Observations on the Nature of Civil Liberty* (London, 1776), p. 154.

24 Ibid., pp. 15–16.

parliamentary sovereignty, whether in the colonies or at home. He also repeated Burgh's attacks on the pretensions of parliamentary representation. In its present state, he suggested, the elective franchise was 'nothing but a power, lodged in a few, to choose at certain periods a body of *masters* for themselves and for the rest of the community'.[25] Even if such a system gave the impression of freedom in people's private lives, it would be 'an abuse of language' to call it liberty – for it depended on the whims of the true rulers, the oligarchy.

Price described the lack of liberty, again like Burgh, as 'slavery'. This was an analogy with deep roots in the ancient Roman classics – a time when chattel slavery was widespread, but not racialised as it was in the eighteenth-century British Empire. When adopted by Americans to describe their own condition under the tyranny of Parliament, the term drew derisive responses from critics who pointed to the horrors of chattel slavery the colonists' economy depended on. The writer Samuel Johnson, a sceptic of both slavery and the case for American independence, wondered in his 1775 pamphlet *Taxation No Tyranny* why the 'loudest yelps for liberty' came from the mouths of slave owners.[26] Responses to Price, too, were keen to point out that his framework did not distinguish between the political slavery of libertyless citizens and the far more brutal slavery imposed on Africans and their descendants in the New World.[27]

What the idea of political slavery was meant to express, though, was the problem of having your own fate rest in someone else's hands. For Price and others like him, that was the true absence of liberty, and – indeed, like chattel slavery – it was not made any less objectionable by a more gracious master or more pleasant conditions. Only by taking an active part in running one's community, by sharing equally in the project of collective self-rule, could citizens experience true freedom. That was a standard the British constitution after 1688 had claimed to meet. Yet it had only ever really done so for a tiny, privileged fraction of the people.

25 Ibid., p. 10.
26 Samuel Johnson, *Taxation No Tyranny* (London, 1775), p. 89.
27 See Skinner, *Liberty as Independence*, pp. 235–6.

Price's book, *Observations on the Nature of Civil Liberty*, made this doctrine of liberty as independence and self-rule available in clear and simple terms, and framed it in the context of the present imperial crisis. Building on the work of those who had drawn parallels between colonial oppression and British domestic tyranny, Price put the case in measured, almost dispassionate prose – as if the sheer force of his argument was bound to shine through by itself. Britain could never put down the Americans by force. But if it did, so much the worse, because a victory in such a cause would be the victory of despotism. The unfolding American revolution was a chance to reckon with the loss of British liberty, a moment for radical transformation on both sides of the Atlantic.

More than any of its predecessors, Richard Price's *Observations* caused shockwaves across British discourse. Within weeks of its publication in February 1776, the society gossip Horace Walpole reported it had 'made a great sensation'.[28] The first edition of 1,000 copies sold out in days, and within a few months total sales were said to have reached nearly 60,000. That was in addition to the extracts printed in several popular newspapers. The book was, apparently, 'universally read'.[29] One sign it struck a nerve was that it garnered so many responses in print. 'All hireling writers were employed to answer', Walpole noted, as Lord North's government rushed to regain control of public opinion. But, of course, attempting to refute Price's arguments also helped draw further attention to them. Already on the back foot militarily, its garrison force besieged in Boston, Britain's establishment was severely shaken.

At the same moment, another piece of writing was causing a similar stir in the colonies themselves. Written and published in the capital of the rebellion, Philadelphia, Thomas Paine's *Common Sense* was a rather different kind of work to Price's *Observations*. For one thing, Paine did

---

28 Cone, *Torchbearer of Freedom*, p. 82.

29 *Lloyd's Evening Post*, 22–4 May 1776, quoted in Yiftah Elazar, 'The Liberty Debate: Richard Price and His Critics on Civil Liberty, Free Government, and Democratic Participation' (PhD diss., Princeton University, 2012), p. 60.

not write in fear of prosecution by British authorities, and so he had no need to couch his rhetoric in terms of loyalty to George III. Nor did he frame his desired revolution as a restoration of some purer version of the British constitution, as both Burgh and Price tended to do. Rather, the shock value of Paine's pamphlet came from his bold assault on every aspect of the British system of government – with its strongest venom reserved for the monarchy itself.

When John Cartwright had first called for 'American independence' in 1774, he had imagined the colonies as 'sister kingdoms' that would continue to pledge their allegiance to the same Crown. Like most of his fellow British thinkers in the commonwealth tradition, he singled out Parliament – with its pretensions to representation and supremacy, as well as its blatant corruption – as the central problem of British politics. Paine, who had spent some time among London political campaigners, was familiar with this approach. In *Common Sense*, though, he unleashed a torrent of searing disdain upon the idea of hereditary rule, clearing the path for a total break between colonies and mother country. His timing was perfect, with British forces fleeing Boston ignominiously that March. By April, many Americans were ready to commit to complete independence.

One of the qualities of *Common Sense* was its ability to speak to ordinary Americans, without devolving into the legalese all too common in political pamphlets of the time.[30] Paine took as his audience not members of legislative assemblies but everyone – all those who had a stake in the future of their communities. It was this sense of universal appeal that Price's *Observations* also shared, and that made it *Common Sense*'s British counterpart. Price handily outsold Paine east of the Atlantic and drew far more attention in the British press. Crucially, his ideas were shared and taken up among the urban working class, circulating well beyond just those who could afford to buy a copy of the book.

---

30 See Robert Ferguson, 'The Commonalities of *Common Sense*', *William and Mary Quarterly* 57, no. 3 (July 2000), pp. 465–504; and Sophia Rosenfeld, 'Tom Paine's *Common Sense* and Ours', *William and Mary Quarterly* 65, no. 4 (October 2008), pp. 633–68.

'Taylors, tallow-chandlers, soap-boilers, [and] chimney-sweepers' were among those influenced by Price's work, according to one conservative critic, not to mention 'traders, mechanics, handicrafts of all kinds', many of them no doubt 'dunces, dotards, and drunkards'. Working men, in other words, and 'female patriots' as well, were the core audience for Price's theory of freedom's true meaning. It was they, after all, who had the most to gain from the kind of political transformation that Price and his fellow thinkers had in mind. 'There is not an apprentice, a drayman, a porter, or shoe-black in town,' went on the author of *Obedience the Best Charter*, 'who does not quote you [that is, Price] for all the extravagant nonsense they utter.'[31] Self-rule for the people and the right to revolution were becoming common sense among the working class in Britain, just as much as they were in America.

While the colonists in Pennsylvania and elsewhere began to craft new, democratic constitutions in the spring of 1776, John Wilkes and his allies in London took their cue from the success of *Observations*. On 21 March, he stood up in Parliament to ask for leave 'to bring in a Bill for the just and equal representation of the people of England'. Citing both Burgh and Price by name, Wilkes argued that the current system was grossly unequal, 'an insult to common sense'. A vote, he said, should be the right of every adult man. 'The meanest mechanic, the poorest peasant and day-labourer', even servants had their lives shaped daily by laws that the legislature made. All of them deserved a share 'in the power of making those laws'. It was every MP's 'duty to the people to restore to them their clear rights', Wilkes declared.[32] If they would not, he said between the lines, the task would lie with the people themselves.

Wilkes's speech, printed in friendly London newspapers, further inflamed the public appetite for political transformation. In the House of Commons, it met with nothing but scornful laughter, except from the tiny group of radicals, such as John Sawbridge and American-born Bristol MP Henry Cruger, who stood with Wilkes. But neither they nor anyone else seriously expected Parliament to take up his populist

---

31 [J. Moir,] *Obedience the Best Charter* (London, 1776), p. 98.
32 *Public Advertiser*, London, 25 March 1776, p. 2.

programme – at least, not without being forced into it by serious threats from the streets. Wilkes's real audience was those outside the chamber, the movement he had cultivated ever since he burst onto the public scene over a decade earlier.

When James Aitken first came to London in 1772, he had paid scant attention to the emerging politics of labour and class struggle in the city, or to high-flown arguments about rights and representation. In Philadelphia, he encountered revolutionary artisans from the perspective of a loyal British subject, born and bred – and got his share of abuse for it, too. Yet, by the time he left London in the spring of 1776, something had changed in Aitken's attitude. The air of crisis was inescapable that winter. And it was ordinary men like him who felt the call to action on behalf of liberty. When he spoke of his reading later, Aitken said he had 'always entertained the highest opinion' of Price's *Observations*. A copy was found among possessions he left behind on the run.[33]

Aitken was just one of many who took inspiration from the visions of a better, freer world offered by Price and other writers. What made him different was not his engagement with revolutionary theory, but his attempt to put it into practice at the heart of Britain's empire.

---

33 [James Aitken,] *Life of James Aitken* (Winchester, 1777), p. 14; *General Evening Post*, 6 February 1777.

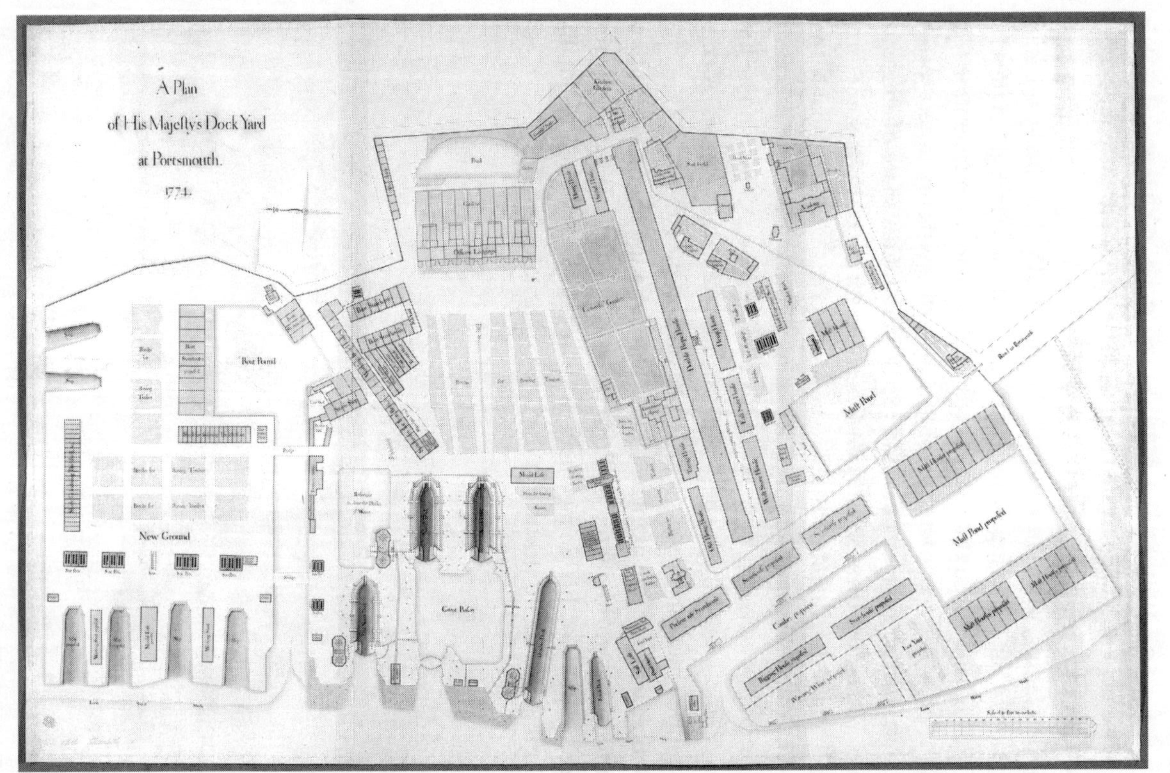

A Plan of His Majesty's Dock Yard at Portsmouth, 1774 (British Library Collection: Maps K.Top.14.45.2)

6

Practice

As winter fell at the end of 1775, the inhabitants of London – including twenty-three-year-old James Aitken – learned the news of a campaign of terror perpetrated by their government against the rebellious colonists in North America. Admiral Thomas Graves had already made known his desire to 'lay waste and destroy' New England's seaport towns, whose citizens had so often humiliated customs men and navy officers alike.[1] Then orders came from London that he was to hold back nothing in his efforts to crush the rebellion. That October, Graves dispatched a squadron to sail up the New England coast, burning towns and harbours as they went. His primary aim was to cripple American maritime infrastructure.

In the event, bad weather intervened. Only the town of Falmouth (precursor of today's Portland, Maine) was actually firebombed. Warned to flee, the townspeople escaped with their lives, if not with their property intact. Americans saw the act as a new low in the chronicle of British tyranny. George Washington, in charge of the new rebel army, declared it 'an outrage exceeding in barbarity and cruelty every hostile act

---

1 Donald Yerxa, 'The Burning of Falmouth, 1775: A Case Study in British Imperial Pacification', *Maine History* 14, no. 3 (1965), p. 120.

practised among civilized nations'.[2] In New England newspapers, Falmouth's destruction was held up as proof of the British ministry's determination, 'with fire and sword, to butcher and destroy, beggar and enslave the whole American people'.[3]

Within months, the British Army was forced to withdraw altogether from the rebellious colonies. It left behind a battered and bruised city of Boston, and the smouldering wreckage of neighbouring Charlestown, set alight by British soldiers during their assault on Bunker Hill. If defeat at Boston showed the fragility of Britain's occupying army, though, it also underscored the importance of British naval supremacy. So long as they were masters of the sea, it would be in the power of the king's forces to strike at almost any point along the vast American coast. Trade would be cut off, which meant supplies of arms and gunpowder would never make it to the rebel army. If the British were to win the war, observers on both sides understood, their victory would be secured at sea.

All this would soon strike Aitken with the force of revelation. When he left London in the spring of 1776, perhaps even then carrying his copy of Richard Price's *Observations*, he seems to have had no more in mind than to explore more of the country. Having spent so much time on the road in the colonies, and then in his journey south from Liverpool, Aitken had grown comfortable with a sort of vagrant lifestyle. For perhaps the next six months, he wandered from London to Cambridge, from Cambridge to Colchester, and then back via London to the coastal towns of Hampshire, where the Royal Navy's warships were a frequent sight, towering above the smaller shipping. It was at his next stop, Oxford, that the idea came to him that was to shape the rest of his life.

By then, the imperial crisis had accelerated into full-blown civil war and revolution. Pushed along by the success of Thomas Paine's explosive polemic, as well as by the hard-line Pennsylvania militiamen who helped put pressure on the delegates in Congress, the rebels had at last published their Declaration of Independence – a final, formal severing of ties

2 George Washington to John Hancock, 24 October 1775; Founders Online.
3 Yerxa, 'Burning of Falmouth', pp. 149–50.

between the colonists and Britain.[4] Those who remembered Falmouth would not have been surprised by the Declaration's charge that George III had 'plundered our seas, ravaged our coasts, burnt our towns, and destroyed the lives of our people'. Indeed, like Washington months earlier, Congress claimed that the British government had shown a 'cruelty and perfidy scarcely paralleled in the most barbarous ages'. Their conduct, the Declaration's authors claimed, was 'totally unworthy . . . of a civilized nation'.[5]

Two of the Declaration's most famous complaints now serve as reminders that the revolutionary states rested on twin foundations of conquest and slavery. When Congress charged that George III had 'excited domestic insurrections amongst us', it was pointing to the promise that Virginia governor Lord Dunmore had made in November 1775 to the colony's fighting-age enslaved men: join the royal army and be granted freedom. When it then claimed that British agents had 'endeavoured to bring on the inhabitants of our frontiers, the merciless Indian savages', it ignored the fact that Indigenous peoples fought to honour their long-standing treaties and defend the homelands settlers coveted. What Congress wanted to convey was that in this war, Britain had already broken all the rules. That was just another reason independence was, at this point, unavoidable.

So, in Oxford that summer, Aitken found himself 'in conversation concerning the American war'. Whether the people he was talking to were sympathetic to the rebel cause we cannot tell, for what interested Aitken at that moment were questions of strategy, not principle or loyalty. That August, a British force arriving by sea had driven the rebel army out of New York city, repaying the blow landed in Boston and

---

4 For the process and politics behind the Declaration of Independence, see William Hogeland, *Declaration: The Nine Tumultuous Weeks When America Became Independent, May 1–July 4 1776* (Simon & Schuster, 2010).

5 Declaration of Independence, 4 July 1776; US National Archives. Within months of the Declaration, the Continental Army was to engage in its own act of strategic arson at New York: see Benjamin Carp, 'The Night the Yankees Burned Broadway: The New York City Fire of 1776', *Early American Studies* 4, no. 2 (Fall 2006), pp. 471–511; Carp, *The Great New York Fire of 1776: A Lost Story of the American Revolution* (Yale University Press, 2023).

sending the city up in flames in the process. What Aitken and his companions could agree on was that the war hinged on sea power. 'His Majesty's fleet and dockyards', they concluded, were essential to 'the safety, the welfare, and even the existence of this nation'.[6] For Aitken, the observation seemed to bring the situation into sudden focus.

'It is amazing,' he later marvelled, 'with what force this conversation kept possession of my mind. I believe it never left me afterwards.' That night he lay restlessly, constructing and reciting a litany of scenarios. 'I had a thousand ideas', he said, and they all pointed in one direction. What if someone could destroy the dockyards, and knock out the Royal Navy in a single blow? 'How important would be the event in favour of America', if something like that were to happen? The more he thought about it, the more it seemed that such a thing might just be possible. This was not a complex or sophisticated plan. It was, avowedly, a young man's fantasy. Yet Aitken did not stop there. Two days later, he began the work of undertaking his 'heroic enterprise'.[7]

As reckless and absurd as this idea might seem, James Aitken took it seriously. He set out to wage a covert war on Britain's military machine. His goal was to put an end to the empire's campaign of repression against the revolutionary American republics, in effect securing independence. This was not intended to be simply some glorious failure, destined to grant the young man his five minutes of notoriety. It was meant, he insisted, to succeed – and he took every step that he could think of to make sure it did.

From Oxford, Aitken journeyed back south to Portsmouth, the home of the kingdom's largest and most crucial naval dockyard. Having passed through Portsmouth and Southampton some weeks earlier, Aitken already had a rough sense of the area. But this time, he came with a sense of purpose. Taking a job with a house painter in nearby Titchfield – a more sustainable source of income, and far better cover, than his

---

6 [James Aitken,] *Life of James Aitken* (Winchester, 1777), pp. 22–3.
7 Ibid., p. 23.

accustomed vagrant lifestyle – he began to gather information on the dockyard. 'I frequently attended the yard, [and] acquainted myself with every part of it', he later boasted. 'I took account of all the ships of war in the harbour, their force, and their number of men.'[8] Over time, he sketched the layout, assessed the fortifications, and noted the patterns of the guards. He was growing increasingly convinced his plan could work.

Portsmouth, however, was not Aitken's sole target. British naval infrastructure was dispersed across several key sites around the south coast, and he intended to hit all of them if possible. Travelling west from Portsmouth, his next destination was Plymouth, on the Devon coast, where he recalled, 'I placed myself in the way of all business, learnt the particulars of everything that was going forward, and examined the contents of every storehouse.'[9] Then he recrossed the south of England and made similar covert inspections of facilities at Chatham, Deptford, and Woolwich, on the Thames. By the end of his tour, Aitken believed he had a thorough knowledge of the places where Britain's warships were built and maintained.

Ideally, at this point, Aitken hoped to bring both his information and his plan to the attention of Congress in Philadelphia. He soon found crossing the Atlantic would be almost impossible – America was subject to a total naval blockade. But Aitken also knew that by the summer of 1776, the American Revolution had come to Europe. Specifically, it had done so in the form of Silas Deane, a Connecticut merchant and congressman whom the rebels had dispatched to France. Aitken determined that Deane was the man to meet. Fearing suspicion if he crossed the Channel by the packet ship, he contracted with some smugglers in Dover to ferry him across alone. Once ashore in Calais, he set off again on foot for Paris. By now, it was already late autumn.

Silas Deane was thirty-eight years old, a prosperous Yale graduate who worked as a lawyer before entering commerce. He married well not once but twice and entered the Connecticut assembly at thirty-two. His task as the unofficial revolutionary ambassador in France was to

---

8 Ibid., p. 24.
9 Ibid., p. 25.

coordinate with sympathisers who could help supply both cash and arms for the cause. It was Deane who, later that year, would enlist the young Marquis de Lafayette as a major general in George Washington's army. While the French royal government remained officially aloof until a treaty of alliance in 1778, Louis XVI's officials hoped that nurturing the rebel cause would wound their British rivals and help redress the balance of global power. Deane's job was to be an opportunist on behalf of the fragile revolution.[10]

When Aitken turned up at his apartments, Deane was not initially impressed. The young man was stooped and lean by American standards, with red hair and a face covered in freckles. He wore shabby clothes that would hardly have passed muster in a market town, let alone Paris. Deane's servant suggested he be turned away without an audience. Yet there was something about this strange man that had caught the American's attention. He decided to let Aitken speak.

Before he began to lay out his scheme, or to hand over the intelligence he had spent months gathering, Aitken gave Deane a sort of test. 'If a man is ill-used,' he asked, 'has he not a right to resent it and to seek revenge or retaliation on those who have injured him?' It was an odd question, but Deane seemed to grasp what the young man was getting at.

'Go into the fields and tread on the meanest insect,' he replied, 'and see if it do not at least try to turn upon you . . . This is the voice [of] the law of nature extending through all her animal creation.'

That was what Aitken wanted to hear. He seemed to take it as a sign that, under everything, the two men answered to the same philosophy of liberty and justice. Perhaps it was America itself Aitken was testing. If so, it was a test the new nation passed.

'Right, right', Deane recalled Aitken responding, 'his eyes sparkling and wild'.[11]

10 Deane's biography is summarised in Julian Boyd, 'Silas Deane: Death by a Kindly Teacher of Treason?', *William and Mary Quarterly* 16, no. 2 (April 1959), pp. 165–87; and Elizabeth Covart, 'Silas Deane, Forgotten Patriot', *Journal of the American Revolution*, 30 July 2014.

11 Silas Deane to Edward Bancroft, March 1777, in *Collections of the New-York Historical Society for the Year 1887* (New York Historical Society, 1888), p. 10.

Over the course of two meetings, Aitken then set out his proposal to destroy the British dockyards. He showed Deane his plans and sketches and explained the incendiary device he claimed to have invented that would allow him to set fires on a sort of timer, so he could escape before they took hold. 'I will strike a blow, ay, such a blow,' said Aitken, 'as will need no repetition.'[12] Deane was sceptical. But he was also, in the end, an opportunist. He asked Aitken how much money he would need – the answer was just enough to get him back to England and to pay for making his devices. In addition to the money, Deane arranged a passport from the French to make sure Aitken was not stopped on the way back. And he told him the name of a man in London who might help.

None of this, Deane emphasised, was to be taken as official sanction on the part of the United States for Aitken's planned activities. He was to maintain total secrecy, sharing his mission with nobody but the agent in London. If the plan were to get out, Deane said, it could do as much damage to the cause as burning down Portsmouth dockyard would do to the British. What Deane did not do, though, was tell Aitken to stand down. From that point on, even if only unofficially, Aitken believed he had the backing of the revolutionary government.

Britain's royal dockyards were crucial foundations of its naval power, and thus of its entire global empire. They were also among Britain's largest employers, sites of labour that, in the eighteenth century, were at the forefront of emerging industrial practices. More than 7,000 men worked in the dockyards on the eve of the American Revolution – and likely a number of women, too. Mary Lacy spent most of her adulthood working at dockyards under the male alias William Chandler, completing an apprenticeship and passing her shipwright's exam in 1770. Soon after, she retired from the trade on account of ill health, won a pension from the admiralty, and wrote a memoir called *The Female Shipwright*. Like the men she worked with, Lacy possessed skills and knowledge that were

12 Ibid., p. 11.

hard to replace. She knew how much her labour was worth, with the power of the navy resting on it.[13]

In the 1770s, however, imperial administrators were eager for cost-cutting efficiencies. The dockyards themselves underwent extensive renovation and expansion in the years before war in America broke out. In Portsmouth, that was partly spurred by a destructive fire in 1770, the origins of which remained mysterious. As capital costs soared, admiralty bosses hoped to balance them with cuts to the cost of labour. They did so by switching workers to a task-work system, paying for specific jobs priced in advance rather than daily wages. At first, task rates were imposed only on more easily replaceable workers. When it was brought in for shipwrights in 1775, however, the workers at Portsmouth went on strike. Describing task work as 'slavery', and themselves as an 'oppressed people', they refused to enter the yard until the admiralty backed down and made the system voluntary.[14]

This background of industrial unrest was part of the reason why, when James Aitken started turning up around the dockyard the following summer, asking questions and snooping around storehouses, none of the workers was particularly keen to stop him. When he returned to Portsmouth in December 1776, after his visit to Silas Deane in Paris, they remained in no rush to raise the alarm. Watchmen at the dockyard gate tended to be former dockyard men themselves, who had got past the age of being useful with their arms and hands. Even when they did see

13 Mary Lacy, *The Female Shipwright* (National Maritime Museum, 2008 [1777]); and see Jen Manion, *Female Husbands: A Trans History* (Cambridge University Press, 2020), pp. 87–93. On dockyards as industrial employers, see Peter Linebaugh, *The London Hanged: Crime and Civil Society in the Eighteenth Century* (Cambridge University Press, 1992), pp. 371–401; Henry Snow, *Enemies of Order: Labor and Power at the Atlantic Dockside* (University of Georgia Press, forthcoming).

14 Snow, *Enemies of Order*, ch. 5. See James Haas, 'The Introduction of Task Work into the Royal Dockyards, 1775', *Journal of British Studies* 8, no. 2 (May 1969), pp. 44–68; Roger Knight, 'From Impressment to Taskwork: Strike and Disruption in the Royal Dockyards, 1688–1788', in Kenneth Lunn and Ann Day, eds, *History of Work and Labor Relations in the Royal Dockyards* (Mansell, 1999), pp. 1–20.

Aitken, what they saw was just another scruffy lad like all the others, on his way to earn a day's wage.

It was a good thing security was lax, for Aitken was hardly an accomplished operator when it came to the practical matter of sabotage. He was comfortable and competent as an observer of the dockyards. It was probably the quantity of information he had gathered that did most to convince Deane that the gambit might be worth his while. In the matter of actually setting things on fire, though, Aitken proved far less capable. Although the danger to himself and others was quite real, his repeated stumbles had the quality of farce.

Aitken knew that Portsmouth would have fire engines – effectively pumps on carts, with hoses that could jet water hundreds of feet – poised to respond to any threat to the precious dockyard. So, his plan involved setting two decoy fires in town, thus distracting the fire crews before the real attack. To this end, he contracted for lodgings in two different places. Then he went to the dockyard and made preparations to start fires in both the hemp-house and the rope-house – well-chosen locations that should certainly burn nicely. But he could not get his flint to strike a light, and ended up getting himself locked in the rope-house. After banging on the doors for some time, he found someone to let him out and went straight to his lodgings and to bed. It was a poor first day as an incendiary.

In the morning, things hardly got better. Aitken's attempt to start a fire in his rooms created such a smell that the landlady came upstairs and threw him out. He deemed it prudent not to make a fuss. After that, he returned to the dockyard, where, apparently, nobody had disturbed his preparations from the day before. This time, he managed to light the makeshift fuse he had constructed in the rope-house and the lantern-like incendiary device that he had hidden in the hemp. This latter was made to his careful designs by an apprentice smith in Canterbury – Aitken's father, a skilled locksmith, would have been appalled at the construction, and it turned out not to take effect. On his way out, Aitken crossed paths with someone who recognised him. Without going back to town to start his decoy fires or retrieve his bundle of possessions, Aitken ran.

Only later did he realise that the fire in the rope-house had, in fact, caught. He was riding in the back of a cart heading north, and when the driver stopped to water her horse – still only a few miles outside Portsmouth – he took the chance to look back towards the dockyard. It was ablaze. When Aitken saw the orange glow, the flicker of flame, and smoke pouring up into the late-afternoon sky, he 'jumped out of the cart without saying a word' and ran on another four miles.[15] Surely, he thought, after all the blunders he had made, someone would be pursuing him. He had succeeded in setting fire to the kingdom's largest dockyard. Could he really have done it and got away?

While dockyard workers gathered to tackle the huge blaze in the rope-house, soon joined by sailors and marines who rowed ashore from warships anchored nearby, James Aitken sped north-east towards London. He was exultant, agitated, terrified, and mentally exhausted. When a passing carriage failed to stop for him, he fired his pistol in a fit of sudden rage – another blunder that could easily have got him caught. But, as he kept walking, Aitken began to calm down. Once he reached London, he would melt into the urban mass as he had done before. What was more, he remembered, Silas Deane had given him the details of an agent in the city. From there, once he had made his report and picked up more cash, he could move on to the next step in his master plan.

Edward Bancroft was a New Englander who, for a short while, had been a student of Deane's in Connecticut. Apprenticed to a physician, at eighteen he ran off to Surinam – a Dutch colony on the South American coast – and learned his practice as a doctor attending enslaved plantation workers. Extending his attention to natural science, especially the wonders of electric eels, Bancroft travelled to London in 1766 and soon became a fixture of the city's scientific scene. Ten years later, Bancroft was thirty years old, a respectable family man and a member of the prestigious Royal Society. When his old teacher

---

15 [Aitken,] *Life*, p. 44.

turned up in Paris that summer with plans to help win independence for the colonies, Bancroft agreed to play his part. He began sending newspapers and reports to keep Deane up to date with affairs in the metropolis.[16]

Bancroft lived at 4 Downing Street, across the road from the prime minister, Lord North. When Aitken turned up at the door, fresh from a wash and a drink in a Westminster pub, he was ushered quickly to a parlour. There Aitken gave his report – 'that I had set Portsmouth dock on fire, which was then in flames' – and told Bancroft he needed more money and somewhere to lie low for a while. The reply he got came as a blow. Bancroft told him that he was indeed good friends with Deane, but he knew nothing of this plot. As someone who lived under British government, he could have no part in such an attack on it. Aitken was stunned and angry, but what could he do? Sharing a few choice words on loyalty, he simply got up and left.

What Bancroft naturally did not mention to Aitken was that he was not the friend Deane thought he was. As soon as he returned from meeting Deane in Paris that past summer, Bancroft was approached by another old friend – a man called Paul Wentworth, who owned property in Surinam and had connections to New Hampshire's royal governor. Wentworth, it turned out, was part of a government spy ring run by an ambitious young MP and civil servant, William Eden.[17] With the promise of a hefty stipend, and no doubt some countervailing threats, Wentworth recruited Bancroft to serve as a double agent for the British government. He passed along any information that he gleaned from correspondence with Deane, helping to undermine the covert American diplomatic effort from the start.

Aitken's appearance at Bancroft's house threatened this delicate arrangement. Clearly, Deane had given the doctor's identity away to a potentially unstable young man, telling him that he would find assistance

---

16 For a sympathetic account of Bancroft's life and activities, which absolves him of the charge of treachery to the United States, see Thomas Schaeper, *Edward Bancroft: Scientist, Author, Spy* (Yale University Press, 2011).

17 Alan S. Brown, 'William Eden and the American Revolution' (PhD diss., University of Michigan, 1953).

at the Downing Street house. Bancroft told Aitken the truth when he said he was content with British rule and had no wish to harm the government he lived under. But he could not bring what he learned about the Portsmouth fire to his handlers without raising awkward questions about his involvement. For his part, Aitken regretted telling Bancroft anything. Before he left London, he sent the doctor a note threatening to name him as an accomplice if anything got to the authorities. The two men therefore had each other in a bind. For the time being, they had to rely on each other's secrecy.

London proved a disappointing refuge. Without the support he counted on, Aitken's plans seemed more precarious than ever. But, if anything, the encounter with Bancroft increased his sense of the righteousness of his cause. He was determined to go on and carry out the plan as he had first imagined it in Oxford. Bancroft, with his comfortable home and family, may have been happy to accept things as they were. Many others, Aitken knew, were not. He was himself among them. Just as Richard Price had argued, revolution in America concerned more than the fate of the colonists themselves. It was a struggle to redeem the promise of British liberty.

After Portsmouth, Aitken's next target was the dockyard at Plymouth, nearly 200 miles to the west. Britain's second most important naval base by the mid-eighteenth century, Plymouth was home to the Western Squadron, whose main duty was the crucial defence of the English Channel. New outer walls had been built three years earlier as part of the admiralty's general programme of improvements. Morale, however, was no better there than in Portsmouth. In their struggle against the new task-work system in 1775, Plymouth shipwrights complained it amounted to 'progressive suicide on our bodies'.[18] They, too, went on strike until it was withdrawn.

By the time Aitken arrived in Plymouth, travelling in short stages and often by foot to avoid detection, it was nearly the end of December. Dockyard authorities had ample time to hear about the disaster at Portsmouth and ramp up security. When Aitken tried to enter through

18 Haas, 'The Introduction of Task Work', p. 58.

the main gate, as he had done easily enough before, he was politely turned back. Now he had to improvise. Walking 'several times round the walls, which are everywhere so high', he realised his only chance would be to scale them, so he spent the next day making a rope ladder to serve the purpose.[19] Yet every time he got over the wall and made his way towards the storehouses he was spooked by the sound of guards. He was clumsy and on edge, as he had been in Portsmouth – but this time, the dockyard was thoroughly locked down.

After several days of trying, Aitken gave up and headed out of town. If he had ended his mission there, he might well never have been caught.

At its genesis, James Aitken's plan to strike the British Empire from within rested on his assessment that the royal dockyards were both linchpins and weak points in the edifice of imperial power. Only the transoceanic reach of its navy allowed Britain to wage war on the former colonies, and to project force in all corners of the world. Smash the dockyards, he reasoned, and British maritime power would collapse – the American campaign with it.

As the new year began, however, Aitken was forced to confront some awkward facts. First, the dockyards were no longer undefended. He had only had one free shot, and he had taken it. Second, there might be more to the British naval infrastructure than just the official navy dockyards. Were not the trading ports that served far larger volumes of shipping equally central to the working of empire? When state capacity was based on the profits of commerce, perhaps it was possible to cut the sinews of power. Having failed at Plymouth, Aitken had to make a new assessment of the situation. Rather than cut his losses and perhaps try to return to Deane in Paris, he decided to select a new target.

In fact, he already had one in mind. Aitken had passed through Bristol on his way from London to Plymouth and had seen for himself the scale of its maritime commerce. For much of the century, Bristol had been losing ground to other cities – including Liverpool, which already

19 [Aitken,] *Life*, p. 49.

handled more shipping. Still, it remained one of a small handful of key centres of ocean-going trade. Each year, the harbour received thousands of tons of sugar grown, cut, and processed by enslaved workers on Caribbean plantations. War in North America hit the city's export trade hard, but it was the Caribbean where most of its imports originated. And while the plantation economy thrived, so did the trade in enslaved people themselves. Bristol merchants, shipbuilders, and suppliers profited from the trade, and those profits, in turn, helped build the city.[20]

Partly for self-interested reasons, fearing the disruption of trade, Bristol's citizens were staunch opponents of the government's aggressive policy towards the colonies. The two MPs they elected in 1774, Edmund Burke and Henry Cruger, both came out strongly against Lord North's government, and even when fighting began in 1775 there was a strong current of support for the American cause. On Friday 13 December 1776, a government-mandated day of fasting and prayer for the rebellion's end, Burke's local supporters held a public dinner as a form of counter-protest, raising a toast to 'the people of Britain, that they may see through the dangerous designs of their arbitrary ministers'.[21] While many wealthier Bristolians gradually abandoned their American sympathies, the city's working class never did. As in other cities, the conflict over liberty in the empire intensified existing class-based struggle over liberty at home.[22]

Aitken blundered into this situation on the rebound from his failure in Plymouth, and apparently with little thought about the difference between attacking a military installation and one of Britain's largest urban centres, home to more than 50,000 people. Arriving in January 1777, he adapted the tactics he had aimed to use in Portsmouth

20 Kenneth Morgan, 'Bristol and the Atlantic Trade in the Eighteenth Century', *English Historical Review* 107 (July 1992), pp. 626–50; Morgan, 'Bristol West India Merchants in the Eighteenth Century', *Transactions of the Royal Historical Society* 3 (December 1993), pp. 185–208.

21 P.J. Marshall, *Bristol and the American War of Independence* (Bristol Branch of the Historical Association, 1977), p. 6.

22 For Bristol's radical working class, see James E. Bradley and Elizabeth Baigent, 'The Sources of Late Eighteenth-Century English Radicalism: Bristol in the 1770s and 1780s', *English Historical Review* 124 (October 2009), pp. 1075–108.

– decoy fires set in residential areas so that his real target, the harbour's ships and warehouses, had time to burn before the fire crews arrived. Once again, though, things immediately started going wrong. He had to abandon some possessions at his lodgings when smoke from his room attracted attention. Two out of the three fires he set on merchant ships failed to catch, while the other did less damage than he hoped. Observing the outcome the next morning, Aitken was 'vexed'.[23]

City authorities were now alert to the danger of arson. A close watch was set on the shipping, and although Aitken did manage one abortive effort to ignite a stack of barrels on the quay, he soon decided the whole area was too risky. Frustrated, the young man then let his anger and self-importance run away with him. He decided that 'the only effectual method I could take to accomplish my business, would be to set the whole town on fire'.[24] He identified more than a dozen warehouses around the city, and at two o'clock on a Sunday morning he went from one to the next with his matches and home-made incendiary devices. By the time the sun was coming up, he was three miles out of town. When he turned to look back, he later recalled, it seemed as if the whole sky was in flames.

Rather than carry on his way out of Bristol, Aitken turned around and went to survey 'the destruction [he] had wrought'.[25] He was disappointed. Only one of the warehouse fires had really taken, spreading in the neighbourhood of Quay Lane; the others had all failed. Nobody died, but several people lost their homes and others a good deal of property. Now, of course, the citizens were truly in uproar. It was clear that somebody, perhaps an organised conspiracy, was trying to destroy them. They had come perilously close, as one newspaper correspondent put it, to a 'general conflagration of this city, the loss of many lives, and the total ruin of thousands'.[26] Volunteers were organised to mount patrols in the

---

23 [Aitken,] *Life*, p. 55.
24 Ibid., p. 56.
25 Ibid., p. 57.
26 *Hampshire Chronicle*, 27 January 1777, quoted in Jessica Warner, *John the Painter: The First Modern Terrorist* (Profile, 2004), p. 153.

streets, in addition to the watchmen on the harbour. Aitken soon concluded any further action was impossible, for now.

It is unclear how Aitken hoped things would go next. As he told it, he left Bristol fully intent on continuing the general plan of sabotage. Woolwich, Deptford, and Chatham were all still on his list, after all. Yet he was out of money, and his first aim was to get to Paris and report to Deane. He thought the American would be pleased with what he had accomplished. In the meantime, shock and terror spread fast through the British press, as well as through the military and government. A manhunt was already underway. He did not know it yet, of course, but as he made his way eastwards through the frost that January, Aitken was taking his last steps as a free man.

John Fielding presiding at his Bow Street
magistrates' court (Wellcome Collection)

7
Captivity

In February 1754, the crowd at Tyburn was in a raucous mood as it assembled in the snow to witness the hanging of Joshua Kidden, a watchmaker's son and former navy man fallen on hard times. Convicted of robbing a young woman as she rode a cart between Tottenham and London, Kidden was just one of the thousands of poor men and women executed in the eighteenth century for crimes against private property. Protesting his innocence to the last, Kidden died on the gallows like any number of other housebreakers, highwaymen, footpads, and thieves – people, in other words, who had a lot in common with the young James Aitken twenty years later.

Except that, as it turned out, Kidden really was innocent. Authorities discovered two years afterwards that he had been the victim of thief-takers: working-class entrepreneurs who aimed to profit from a war on crime that Britain's ruling class had been trying to wage since the 1740s. One of these gangs' favoured tactics was to find stooges and set them up for crimes, pocketing the reward-money offered by the Crown when a conviction was secured. Stephen McDaniel and his crew had been engaged in such activities for years when they were finally caught out and tracked down by a magistrate from Kent. He and two associates were sentenced to death for Kidden's murder, though none were in fact executed. One of them was Mary Jones, the woman in the cart.[1]

This kind of abuse was one outcome of a system that, for much of the eighteenth century, relied on criminal networks to do most of the work of pursuing justice. Even before the Kidden scandal, there were plenty of people who believed a new approach was needed. One of them was the novelist Henry Fielding, a magistrate based on Bow Street in Westminster – and biographer of the infamous 'thief-taker general', Jonathan Wild.[2] Fielding had persuaded the government to pay for a small force of, effectively, professional police officers, to work out of Bow Street investigating crimes and tracking down suspects. After Henry died and his half-brother John Fielding took over in 1754, the operation expanded and began to get publicity. The men at Bow Street, it seemed, had invented a new type of policing.[3]

John Fielding certainly looked the part. Blind since an accident at the age of nineteen, he presided over court proceedings with a black sash over his eyes like a living embodiment of justice itself. He was also relentlessly energetic in both developing and promoting the Bow Street brand of law enforcement: recruiting officers, adopting new methods of pre-trial investigation, and expanding the reach of his networks first into the rest of London, then the country as a whole. The 1755 pamphlet *A Plan for Preventing Robberies Within Twenty Miles of London* gave an early sense of Fielding's ambition. His government patron, the Duke of

1 Tim Hitchcock and Robert Shoemaker, *London Lives: Poverty, Crime, and the Making of a Modern City* (Cambridge University Press, 2015), pp. 225–8. For the practice of thief-taking, see Ruth Paley, 'Thief-Takers in London in the Age of the McDaniel Gang, c.1745–1754', in Douglas Hay and Francis Snyder, eds, *Policing and Prosecution in Britain, 1750–1850* (Oxford University Press, 1989), pp. 301–41.

2 Henry Fielding, *The Life and Death of Jonathan Wild, the Great* (London, 1743).

3 See J.M. Beattie, 'Sir John Fielding and Public Justice: The Bow Street Magistrates' Court, 1754–1780', *Law and History Review* 25, no. 1 (Spring 2007), pp. 61–100; F.M. Dodsworth, 'The Idea of Police in Eighteenth-Century England: Discipline, Reformation, Superintendence, c.1780–1800', *Journal of the History of Ideas* 69, no. 4 (October 2008), pp. 583–604; Beattie, *The First English Detectives: The Bow Street Runners and the Policing of London, 1750–1840* (Oxford University Press, 2012).

Newcastle, was delighted with the initiative. In 1761, at age forty, Fielding was knighted for his services.

In one sense, Fielding's techniques were not as much of a departure from past practice as he liked to claim. Many of the officers he employed, especially early on, had close links to existing thief-takers and their networks. Like other magistrates before him, Fielding traded heavily in favours and threats in his efforts to get information or put witnesses on the stand. Yet his approach did point towards a new kind of policing system, one that served as an arm of the centralised executive state, rather than part of civic or parish self-government. Reforms enacted over the following century would eventually institutionalise that shift, but not without resistance from people who saw it as another ministerial power-grab: an attack on the same sense of civil liberty that animated British friends of the American Revolution.

Fielding himself had clear views about what society should look like, and what a police force was meant to achieve. Through the 1750s and '60s, he waged campaigns against gambling and prostitution, tried to ban performances of *The Beggar's Opera*, and even raided a pub to shut down 'an illegal meeting of servants and apprentices'.[4] In fact, he was blunt from the outset about the role of policing as a weapon against the working class in general. 'In large and populous cities,' he wrote in a 1758 promotional pamphlet, 'artificers, servants and labourers compose the bulk of the people, and keeping them in good order is the object of the police.'[5] He did not publish his officers' names, because they were so 'obnoxious to the common people' that doing so might put them in danger.[6]

When Aitken arrived in London in 1772 and started mixing with the city's criminal community, he would quickly have become familiar with Fielding and his henchmen. That year, the Bow Street establishment started publishing a journal – the *Quarterly Pursuit* – that listed unsolved

---

4 Hitchcock and Shoemaker, *London Lives*, p. 233.

5 John Fielding, *An Account of the Origin and Effects of a Police Set on Foot by His Grace the Duke of Newcastle in the Year 1753* (London, 1758), p. vii.

6 John Fielding, *A Plan for Preventing Robberies Within Twenty Miles of London* (London, 1755), p. 24.

crimes along with descriptions of the alleged perpetrators. The publication was intended to help circulate information more easily and systematically around the country, helping authorities in one town to identify suspects who might be wanted in another. It is possible Aitken even read about his own audacious highway robberies, prompting his decision to take ship for the colonies. By then, London's crime wave was coming to an end – and Fielding was taking credit.

Since returning to England in 1775, Aitken had spent most of his time outside London. His campaign of incendiary sabotage focused on dockyards (and, eventually, a city) many miles from the great metropolis. He might have thought he was outside Fielding's purview. But there was nobody in Britain more qualified to run a national police investigation: the hunt for the Portsmouth and Bristol arsonists. It was not long before the admiralty came knocking to seek the great man's assistance. Britain, it was now clear, was under attack from an internal enemy. As far as Fielding was concerned, of course, it always had been.

In Portsmouth, all those involved with putting out the rope-house fire began with the assumption that it was an accident. The two men responsible for keeping the place tidy and secure were on the hook, but not for deliberate arson. Also in the line of fire, as it were, was the dockyard commissioner, James Gambier – a navy captain whose connections never quite helped him recover from the fallout of a youthful affair with an admiral's wife. Briefly commodore of the North American station, Gambier was sent to Portsmouth in 1773. It was hardly a plum post for a forty-eight-year-old, and the fire naturally increased his burdens tenfold.[7]

On the upside, Gambier was lucky. Damage to the rope-house and its environs, including the loss of the rigging for two ships under repair at

7 David Syrett, ' "This Penurious Old Reptile": Rear-Admiral James Gambier and the American War', *Historical Research* 74 (February 2001), pp. 63–76; Roger Knight, 'Gambier, James (bap. 1725, d. 1789), Naval Officer', *Oxford Dictionary of National Biography*, 2004.

the time, amounted to some £20,000 – a huge sum, more than double the value of the tea destroyed in Boston harbour by the Sons of Liberty. But it could have been so much worse. If he had not ordered the *Albion*, carrying 2,000 barrels of gunpowder, to put to sea as soon as the alarm was raised (or if the tide had been out and the ship could not escape), Gambier might have been blown to smithereens along with the rest of the dockyard.[8] Once the fire was out, his strategy was to minimise the whole thing as much as he could, writing it off as an unfortunate but ultimately unimportant mishap.

James Aitken's blunders as a saboteur, however, soon made that theory impossible to sustain. A dockyard carpenter came forward, saying he had met someone acting suspiciously. During the clear-up operation, workers found the failed incendiary device Aitken left in the hemp-house. Then there was Elizabeth Boxall, the landlady who threw him out after she smelled smoke coming from his room – it took her a few weeks to come forward, at the urging of her friends. By then, two officers from Bow Street had already been in Portsmouth asking questions. Investigators from the Navy Board were following up leads from the carpenter's account. All this was already underway before Aitken set his one effective fire in Bristol. After that, things escalated very quickly.

Along with the inevitable Bow Street officers, the government dispatched three companies of soldiers to Bristol to keep order. A flurry of suspects were arrested, and the impression reigned that the fires were the work of a widespread conspiracy, not just a single man. The king himself, who had held several meetings on the matter at Buckingham Palace, was reported to have 'expressed the utmost anxiety' for his innocent subjects in Bristol.[9] He offered a royal pardon and a reward of £1,000 to anyone who could give information leading to the perpetrators' capture, a sum to which citizens of Bristol added. At this point, the admiralty put up its own £1,000 reward for

---

8 Jessica Warner, *John the Painter: The First Modern Terrorist* (Profile, 2004), pp. 139–40.

9 *General Evening Post*, 18 January 1777.

information on the Portsmouth fire, advertising details of their suspect in the newspapers. The whole country was now on the hunt for arsonists.

Meanwhile, Aitken himself was hiking through the countryside in the general direction of Dover, hoping to make his way to Paris and Silas Deane. Out of money, he was forced to fall back on his old ways – breaking into roadside shops to steal cash, food, and small items for fencing later. One of those shops was a haberdashery in Calne, a little under thirty miles east of Bristol. There, Aitken made yet another critical mistake: he left behind one of his pair of pistols. When the shopkeeper woke up next morning and discovered both pistol and robbery, he decided to set out in pursuit of the thief himself. This was just a day or two after the Bristol fire and descriptions had not yet reached Calne. The shopkeeper had no idea who he was chasing.

News of the fires and reward had, however, reached Andover, another thirty miles east, by the time Aitken came through towards the end of January. There, the warden of the local bridewell – basically a combination jail and workhouse, where village authorities housed vagrants and petty criminals – kept abreast of the reports and had already read descriptions of the suspect in the Portsmouth arson case. When he heard a neighbour describe a passing vagrant (perhaps with stolen goods to sell) he knew at once who it must be. Both the shopkeeper and the bridewell warden were now hot on Aitken's tail. They caught up with him one or two days later, in the north-Hampshire village of Odiham. If Dover really was his destination, he had made it almost halfway there.

Aitken put up no resistance to his captors. Even if he fought them off and escaped, the fact they had been able to track him down meant others could surely do the same. With more than £2,000 on his head, England was no longer somewhere he could be anonymous. He was, after all, no longer just another burglar or highwayman. Confined in the bridewell at Odiham, Aitken was soon identified by the carpenter from Portsmouth – someone he had tried to exchange friendly words with on the day he set the fire. Once the admiralty knew they had their man, they sent a king's messenger to escort him up to London, along with two of Fielding's officers from Bow Street. By the time he was committed to the New Prison in Clerkenwell, Aitken was in shackles.[10]

Once it became absolutely clear that the fires in Portsmouth and Bristol were not accidental, public discourse leaped to the question of blame. This was a political issue, with room for posturing and insinuation on both sides – but it was undoubtedly a more difficult problem for the friends of America than for its enemies. Edmund Burke knew as much right away. The Bristol MP was no revolutionary, but he had placed himself firmly on the side of reconciliation with the colonies.[11] That presented an opportunity to his opponents in the city, who would latch onto pro-American sentiment as a likely motive for the fire. Sure enough, they blamed 'persons deputed by the Congress in America to distress England'.[12] An American-born sailor was among those rounded up for questioning on day one.

Burke responded with a combination of denial and distancing. At first, he emphasised that fires were common enough at any time, and this one had done relatively little damage. Then he put up his own fifty-guinea reward for information on the 'atrocious offender', and proposed to increase punishments for anyone convicted of even *attempted* arson at dockyards and harbours.[13] Burke's allies in Parliament took a similar approach. Opposition leader Charles Fox dismissed the idea of a nationwide arson conspiracy as an 'improbable story', likely concocted in the hope of putting yet more power in the ministry's hands – and, indeed, Lord North rushed through an Act allowing the detention of suspected traitors without charge.[14] Before long, though, elite friends of America

---

10 Warner, *John the Painter*, pp. 169–73.

11 P.J. Marshall, *Bristol and the American War of Independence* (Bristol Branch of the Historical Association, 1977), pp. 1–6.

12 *General Evening Post*, 18 January 1777.

13 Warner, *John the Painter*, p. 158.

14 Peter Rushton and Gwenda Morgan, *Treason and Rebellion in the British Atlantic, 1685–1800: Legal Responses to Threatening the State* (Bloomsbury, 2020), p. 145.

had a new line. The culprit, they said, was a madman whose motives had nothing to do with them.

It was not only Burke's political rivals who sought to capitalise on public outrage in the wake of the fires. John Wesley, the Methodist clergyman, had already come out against the colonists in a 1775 pamphlet. His follow-up in early 1777 was a direct response to the perceived internal threat. Having argued that the colonists were being misled by 'determined enemies to monarchy' in Britain, who wished to erect 'their dear commonwealth upon its ruins', Wesley now reversed course.[15] It was Britons who had been duped by Americans and their 'talk of liberty', believing they were 'honest, upright men who only withstood oppression'. Now it appeared rebel agents would not scruple to 'burn whole towns, without any regard for the sick and aged' put in danger. God-fearing people should be ashamed 'to speak of them with tenderness', he thundered.[16]

Newspapers in Bristol, London, and elsewhere reported breathlessly on the search for the 'diabolical incendiaries'.[17] Some also speculated on their punishment when brought to justice. Without wishing to seem 'an advocate for cruelty', one correspondent urged that they be burned to death 'by the same raging element wherewith they dare attempt to perpetrate so horrid a crime'.[18] Indeed, although the death-count of the fires was zero, commentators in the British press rushed to describe arson as the worst sin imaginable. Visions of engulfing flame and scorching heat conjured connections to the underworld – to set a fire was hellish, devilish, altogether evil. 'Of all bad characters', one London paper declared, 'an incendiary is the foulest.'[19]

15 John Wesley, *A Calm Address to Our American Colonies* (London, 1775), p. 13.

16 John Wesley, *A Calm Address to the Inhabitants of England, &c.* (London, 1777), pp. 13, 14, 19; see David Morgan, '"The Dupes of Designing Men": John Wesley and the American Revolution', *Historical Magazine of the Protestant Episcopal Church* 44, no. 2 (June 1975), pp. 121–31.

17 *Public Advertiser*, 18 January 1777.

18 *Felix Farley's Bristol Journal*, 25 January 1777, quoted in Warner, *John the Painter*, p. 165.

19 *General Evening Post*, 18 January 1777.

In the face of this onslaught, there was no possibility of a public defence of James Aitken's actions. It was also clear that government took the threat seriously. Under no circumstances would it countenance open support for attacks on the country's navy and shipping. As a result, newspapers most sympathetic to the American cause kept their silence on the arson cases, except to report the facts as they emerged. Men with public profiles, like Burke and Fox, distanced themselves as much as they could from the incidents. 'The poor Americans suffer for it', wrote one of Burke's friends in Bristol, 'as the blame is laid on them. We, therefore, who espouse their cause', he added, were 'not without wretched reflections'.[20] In terms of the struggle for public opinion, Aitken's sabotage campaign was clearly a disaster.

This does not, however, indicate that nobody in Britain harboured secret hopes for the destruction of the navy and American victory in the war. The suspicion that such people did exist is exactly what animated government agents, as well as conservatives like Wesley. That suspicion was also borne out, in small measure at least, by the spate of further incidents that followed the mass public outcry over Aitken's fires. Sources in Exeter claimed they had been 'the object of the dire incendiaries' in multiple attacks, 'though happily with little damage'.[21] Arson was also attempted at dockyards in Harwich and Gravesend. And, on the warship *Terrible*, then docked at Portsmouth, a sailor planted an incendiary device that never took effect.[22] All this came after high security had already been put in place across the country, as others tried to carry on the work that Aitken had begun.

One person who did have an interest in defending such tactics was the man who had effectively enabled them – Silas Deane. Needless to say, Deane did not reveal himself in public. But, in correspondence with a disconcerted Edward Bancroft, he took up the task of justifying covert action. As Deane saw it, the issue was an outdated notion of military honour. Why should it be noble for an admiral to win a battle, but not for

20 Marshall, *Bristol and the American War of Independence*, p. 10.
21 Warner, *John the Painter*, p. 163.
22 Ibid., pp. 163–4.

some agent, 'at equal hazard to his own life', to burn up the enemy fleet before it even set sail? If such an agent could destroy the weapons intended 'to spread devastation and bloodshed in my country', would not doing so save far more lives than winning on the battlefield? Deane was convinced the 'court of common sense' would acquit him of any wrongdoing.[23] That is, if his involvement ever came to light.

James Aitken appeared in Sir John Fielding's courtroom for the first time on 2 February 1777. He was still in chains. Fielding, presumably, wore the trademark black sash over his eyes. As it often was, the court – really the parlour of a Bow Street townhouse, gradually adapted to the purpose over several decades – was full of people. What was unusual was that several of the audience were high-ranking navy officials. Earlier that day, Fielding had met with the Earl of Suffolk, one of Britain's two secretaries of state. There could be no doubt that securing a conviction in the arson cases and uncovering the wider conspiracy that surely lay behind them were a government priority. It was time to demonstrate control of the situation.

The suspect, however, was not cooperating. Despite being identified by men from Portsmouth, he flatly denied that he had ever been either to that town or to Bristol. Aitken knew he had been caught for the robbery in Calne. But he also knew no one had any solid evidence that he had anything to do with the fires. And if he had learned one thing from his housebreaking friends in London, it was to say nothing unless you stood to benefit from saying it. Day after day, Aitken kept his guard up. He replied to Fielding's questions, just not with anything helpful. As one of the more sympathetic newspapers reported it, he 'artfully refused to answer' what was put to him.[24] Others called him sullen. Either way, if it went on much longer it would start to cause some real embarrassment.

---

23 Deane to Bancroft, March 1777, in *Collections of the New-York Historical Society for the Year 1887* (New York Historical Society, 1888), pp. 6–7.
24 Warner, *John the Painter*, p. 177.

Edward Bancroft, the spy, was watching the case especially carefully. He knew there was a good chance the suspect was the same man who had come to see him that night in his Downing Street home – and, if that was the case, there was also a good chance Bancroft's identity would come out. So, he was glad to learn that Aitken had so far 'eluded all important questions'.[25] What worried him was the chance of some sort of deal. Clemency in exchange for his accomplices, say. Any such arrangement would surely put Bancroft in a very delicate situation. Luckily for him, that was not how things played out.

On his visits to Bow Street, Aitken was confronted with a string of witnesses – one of his landladies, the painter who gave him work near Portsmouth, victims of various robberies. These encounters were supposed to show him that the game was up, there was nothing further to be gained from his denials, and he might as well come clean. He never did. But one of the witnesses brought forth to testify struck him as different from the others. First of all, Aitken really had never seen him before. John Baldwin was a Welshman and a house painter who, like Aitken, had spent some time living in Philadelphia. After the questioning, which seemed to go nowhere, the two men contrived to exchange a few words privately. Soon after that, Baldwin began to visit Aitken in his cell at Clerkenwell prison.[26]

The friendship the pair struck up was based on more than just Aitken's loneliness and their shared memories of Philadelphia, for Baldwin soon let Aitken in on a secret. He was not there by accident, he said – he had been sent by the friends of America in England. The plan was to help Aitken break out of prison. Over the next two weeks, they met frequently, and Baldwin began smuggling in tools for the escape attempt. As they planned, Aitken mentioned that he knew Silas Deane, the American agent in Paris, and had got from him a passport to travel through France freely (in fact, he added, he had left it with a bundle of his things in Portsmouth). Maybe Deane would help again, if Baldwin could get him as far as Calais? Perhaps there was hope for Aitken yet.

25 Edward Bancroft to Silas Deane, 7 February 1777, in *Collections of the New-York Historical Society for the Year 1886* (New York, 1887), p. 485.
26 Warner, *John the Painter*, pp. 177–8.

A few days after that conversation, Aitken was back at Bow Street. This time, had he been looking closely, he might have perceived the faintest smile of triumph playing across Fielding's lips. What the magistrate now had in his possession was better than any witness. It was, finally, proof in black and white that there was a conspiracy to burn down Portsmouth royal dockyard – a passport, signed by the French foreign secretary, in the name of one 'James Actzen'. He flourished the document and, sensing his subject had been caught off guard, pressed the attack. Have you ever met a man named Silas Deane? he asked. In that moment, Aitken's artful elusiveness abandoned him. Yes, he admitted, he had met a Silas Deane. Yes, he went on, that man may have given him some money.[27]

In the next day's newspapers, there was general agreement that the final, winning move had now been played. 'Many circumstances came out,' reported the *Public Advertiser*, 'that seem to leave scarce a doubt of his being the incendiary at Bristol and Portsmouth.'[28] It had been more than three weeks since Aitken was brought to London, but at last the government had the hard evidence to put its case before a jury. Aitken knew what had happened, perhaps even from the moment he saw the French passport in Fielding's hand. He was convinced that there was 'nothing sufficiently strong against me to prove guilt' in the arson cases, until he was 'decoyed into a trap set for me by Mr. Baldwin, to whom I disclosed the whole of my proceedings against government'.[29]

While some papers praised Fielding for securing Aitken's downfall, and others gave the credit to Lord Sandwich, the chief of the admiralty, neither of those men was the actual architect of the trap that brought Aitken down. That honour must be reserved for the elderly Richard Grenville, Earl Temple, who had once been a staunch ally of William Pitt and a financial backer of John Wilkes. It was Temple's old connections in the pro-American movement that allowed him to find Baldwin and to brief him properly – which is probably why Temple was approached on

27 Ibid., p. 182.
28 *Public Advertiser*, 25 February 1777, p. 3.
29 [James Aitken,] *Life of James Aitken* (Winchester, 1777), p. 60.

the matter in the first place. So it was in a double sense that Aitken and his cause had been betrayed by those he thought were friends. It was an 'unmanly contrivance', Bancroft observed in his report to Deane. But it succeeded, he wrote, 'before any means to prevent it could be executed'.[30]

One final time, in early March, James Aitken made his way down from London towards the coast. This time, he was chained and under heavy guard. Four officers from Bow Street escorted him for the sixty-five-mile carriage journey. By the end of it, Aitken was famished and exhausted. His destination was Winchester, the county town of Hampshire, where he was due to be put on trial at the spring assizes. Sir John Fielding made his way separately to witness the conclusion of his investigative efforts, and perhaps to manage things behind the scenes. Lord Sandwich and the other admiralty heads also came down to Winchester for the trial. It was to be a grand exhibition of British imperial justice – and, the assembled officials hoped, the end of a challenging ordeal.

There could be little serious doubt about the outcome of the trial, and yet the authorities in London spared no effort or expense. Against Aitken, who, like most defendants at the assizes, would represent himself, were arrayed five prosecutors of varying seniority.[31] The most senior of them all was William Murray, Lord Mansfield, the Lord Chief Justice – and the same man who had reluctantly freed James Somerset from slavery in 1772. Mansfield did not take a major role in the proceedings, but his very presence conveyed in intimidating fashion the full power of the British legal establishment. Both the jury and presiding judges were no doubt suitably overawed.

Aitken's trial took one whole day. For seven hours, he stood in Winchester's medieval Great Hall, as the prosecution lawyers called forth witness after witness – nineteen in all – to place him in Portsmouth at the time of the fire, and connect him to the incendiary device made in Canterbury. By far the longest testimony was that of John Baldwin, who

30 Bancroft to Deane, February 1777, in *Collections . . . for the Year 1887*, p. 3.
31 Warner, *John the Painter*, pp. 192–8.

recounted his conversations with Aitken over the two weeks of their ostensible friendship. It was Baldwin's damning account, on top of the passport itself and the weight of circumstantial evidence, which clinched the case. But what most observers remembered was Aitken's incredible composure. Newspaper reports compared him to Guy Fawkes, who it was said 'displayed the most intrepid firmness, mixed with scorn, and some degree of humour; refusing to discover his accomplices, and showing no concern but for the failure of his enterprise'.[32]

Edward Bancroft, for one, was pleased with the performance. Aitken had resisted all attempts to push him towards naming co-conspirators. While hints about Bancroft's involvement did come out in the press, his British handlers evidently continued to trust him. When he left for France later that month, it was with backing (and a stipend) from the government's spymaster, William Eden.[33] Meanwhile, Silas Deane's support for Aitken's efforts had been thoroughly established. Prosecutors taunted Aitken at the trial with the prospect that his friend Deane, too, would be subject to British justice 'in due time'.[34] Deane himself remained convinced that he had done what common sense dictated for the war effort, regardless of the formal rules of military honour.

Having sat through hours of evidence, and the judge's lengthy summing-up, it took the jury only moments to convict Aitken of setting fire to the Portsmouth rope-house. Because he was never charged for the fires at Bristol, they remained officially unsolved and no one received the hefty rewards offered in their aftermath. Baldwin himself spent years trying to get paid for his critical assistance in the case. In the end, he had to threaten to publish the inside story before he could get anyone to take him seriously – and even then, he only got £100.[35] It was, perhaps, a fair reward for his act of betrayal.

---

32 *Edinburgh Courant*, 12 March 1777, p. 2.

33 Thomas Schaeper, *Edward Bancroft: Scientist, Author, Spy* (Yale University Press, 2011), pp. 80–2.

34 [Anon.,] *The Trial, at Large, of James Hill, Alias John the Painter* (London, 1777), p. 13.

35 Marshall, *Bristol and the American War of Independence*, pp. 11–12.

In his last days, with the hour of his execution drawing near, Aitken turned to reflecting on his life. He had spent such a long time keeping secrets and existing under false names, it was almost a relief to have no further reason to hold back. Even to Baldwin, he had never spoken about anything except the practicalities of his mission and the plan for his escape. So, when men came to visit him in the Winchester jailhouse, wanting to hear everything he had to say, Aitken did not disappoint them. One was a clerk sent by Fielding, who knew there was much more to the story than Aitken had ever let slip under questioning. To buy the jailkeeper's cooperation, Fielding gave him permission to sell a copy of the transcript to be published. Plenty of people, both men knew, would want to hear the story of the great incendiary.[36]

This narrative was, in a sense, Aitken's confession. But it was not really the fires at Portsmouth or Bristol that stirred his sense of guilt. Rather, Aitken used the opportunity to list in detail the harm he had done to individuals: the shops and homes that he had broken into and the items he had stolen. What caused him most shame of all – in fact, the only time he used the word – was what he had done on his way past Basingstoke in late summer, 1776. 'I saw a girl watching some sheep,' the published transcript reads, 'upon whom, with threats and imprecations, I committed a rape, to my shame be it said!'[37] By confessing to the crime now, Aitken could not take back what he had done. He would, though, die having acknowledged it in the face of the world.

On 10 March, four days after his trial, Aitken was taken in a coach to Portsmouth and transferred into a small, two-wheeled cart. This would then convey him to his hanging. With Aitken aboard, the cart first entered the dockyard and was pulled around the whole enormous length of the ruined rope-house. Aitken was frightened now, and rambling. On the way, he stopped the cart to ask forgiveness from James Gambier, the dockyard commissioner. Back outside the dockyard, he spent some time knelt in prayer, then addressed the crowd with formulaic words about God and repentance – at least, that is what was

---

36 Warner, *John the Painter*, pp. 208–11.
37 [Aitken,] *Life*, p. 22.

written down.[38] There were no sympathisers in the crowd who might have heard some bold, dramatic final speech, and, in truth, Aitken was in no fit state to make one.

Near the dockyard gates the mizzen-mast from a warship, the *Arethusa*, had been set up as a gallows. It was over sixty-four feet high. When he had finished praying, Aitken 'was hauled up by a running tackle to the top'.[39] After an hour, the twenty-four-year-old's dead body was brought down and hung in irons at the harbour mouth.

38 Ibid., pp. 62–3; Warner, *John the Painter*, pp. 218–22.
39 Marshall, *Bristol and the American War of Independence*, p. 11.

8

Freedom

British authorities had no time to savour their victory over the diabolical incendiary plot. Even as James Aitken's trial was being prepared and public attention to the case was at its height, news began to trickle into London that would have far greater implications for the outcome of the American war. George Washington's Continental Army, which had spent much of 1776 retreating, was now fiercely contesting the crucial territory between Philadelphia and New York city. Crossing the icy Delaware that Christmas, Washington's force surprised the Hessian mercenaries at Trenton, New Jersey. Eight days later, they routed the British rearguard at Princeton. Suddenly, initiative in the war belonged to the Americans. As the double agent Edward Bancroft reported, 'the loss they have sustained . . . will force the British government to take into its pay more German troops', stretching its credit thin.[1]

In the year that followed, Britain's military position mostly continued to worsen. Even the capture and occupation of the rebel capital at Philadelphia in September proved a remarkably short-lived triumph – for less than a month later, an army of 7,000 men led by the dashing and

---

1 Edward Bancroft to Silas Deane, 13 February 1777, in *Collections of the New-York Historical Society for the Year 1886* (New York, 1887), p. 490.

sophisticated general John Burgoyne was pinned down and captured by Continentals at Saratoga in northern New York. Disagreement over strategy among the British leaders was part of the problem, but just as important was the harassment their troops faced from ordinary colonists in both the New Jersey and New York campaigns. 'America is never to be regained without making an absolute conquest of her', wrote one disillusioned junior commander.[2] Opponents of the war had predicted as much from the outset.

By the end of 1777, as rumours mounted that France would soon enter the war on the side of the American rebels, Lord North and his cabinet began at last to plan for compromise. In fact, North had more than just rumours to go on, because British spies in France – including Bancroft, who had moved to Paris that spring – were reporting regularly on deliberations within Louis XVI's government. The man in charge of that spy network was William Eden, a thirty-two-year-old undersecretary of state with no shortage of vision and ambition. North valued Eden's advice highly, even when it conflicted (as it often did) with that of Lord Stormont, the ambassador to France. What Eden advised, as early as November, was that victory had become unattainable. An acceptable peace should now be the government's aim.

It was not until February 1778 that North was ready to bring such an idea forward publicly. The king had taken considerable convincing and so, he was sure, would Parliament. Eden, shrewd as ever, counselled that waverers could be won over with a distribution of 'honours and favours'.[3] To put a stop to the bloodshed in America, North announced, he was repealing both the duty on tea and the shutdown of the Massachusetts government that had so inflamed rebels' spirits in 1774. He was also appointing a commission of peacemakers, who would be dispatched across the ocean to seek a negotiated settlement with Congress. It would be led by the young Earl of Carlisle, but everyone knew that the real

---

2 William Harcourt to Earl Harcourt, 31 May 1777, quoted in David Hacket Fischer, *Washington's Crossing* (Oxford University Press, 2004), p. 361.

3 William Eden to Frederick North, 7 December 1777, quoted in Alan S. Brown, 'William Eden and the American Revolution' (PhD diss., University of Michigan, 1953), p. 66.

brain of the operation was Carlisle's Eton school friend, Eden. He wrote his own salary for the job – £6,225.[4]

In essence, the offer that the Carlisle Commission brought to Congress in 1778 was a version of the plan of union proposed by Joseph Galloway in Philadelphia four long years earlier. It promised a limitation on Parliament's role in the administration of the colonies, with Congress itself formalised as a collective colonial legislature. At the same time, the colonists were invited to elect Members of Parliament, and to have a greater say in choosing their own governors and customs officers. Taxation was to be voluntary, for purposes of mutual defence only. The Commission was also empowered to suspend any law passed since 1763 that was offensive to the colonists. By the standards of 1775, it was a generous proposal. Yet, diplomatically speaking, Eden's conciliation project was dead on arrival.[5]

Before the commissioners even left England, their prospects of a warm reception in America were dwindling. Confirmation reached London in March of the treaty that Silas Deane – along with his colleagues since late 1776, Benjamin Franklin and Arthur Lee – had negotiated with France. That threw military planning into disarray, as North and his officials tried to work out how to redistribute the empire's resources for another global, inter-imperial war, not only with France but with its ally Spain as well. Franklin, who knew that the momentum was with the rebels, wrote derisively about North's 'little arts and schemes' when they were leaked to him in February. The proposals for conciliation, he was certain, were intended 'to divide and distract us', not offer real progress towards peace.[6]

Prospects for the commissioners did not improve once they set sail aboard the warship *Trident*. Someone cut two crucial ropes while they

---

4 Brown, 'William Eden', p. 101.

5 Anthony Gregory, ' "Formed for Empire": The Continental Congress Responds to the Carlisle Peace Commission', *Journal of the Early Republic* 38, no. 4 (Winter 2018), pp. 643–72. For an analysis suggesting the colonial public might have been open to the Commission's terms, if they had been better known, see Robert Parkinson, *The Common Cause: Creating Race and Nation in the American Revolution* (University of North Carolina Press, 2016), pp. 384–97.

6 Benjamin Franklin to David Hartley, 26 February 1778; Founders Online.

were offshore waiting for good winds, leading Carlisle to wonder if he was sailing with 'another John the Painter' (that is, another James Aitken).[7] Then, soon after they landed in America, they lost another crucial bit of leverage – the new British commander, Sir Henry Clinton, was ordered to transfer forces to combat French and Spanish threats in Florida and the Caribbean. That meant he would have to pull his men out of Philadelphia and concentrate on defending New York. It was as if the rebels had recaptured their capital without needing to fire a shot. In these circumstances, nobody in Congress was inclined to entertain a peace offer on any other terms than total independence.

That May, as they prepared to evacuate Philadelphia, British officers held an extravagant festival at a nearby country estate. The *meschianza*, as they dubbed it, was effectively a celebration of the highly unequal social order British rule had come to represent. Young women from wealthy Philadelphia families played their parts, disguised as Turkish maidens and paraded on horseback by British officers dressed as medieval knights. The enslaved Black women who attended them were also costumed in fashionable oriental style, with silver collars that suggested a sultan's harem. Intended as a gesture towards the refinements that America would lose outside the British Empire, many patriots saw in the *meschianza* all the signs of the very corruption they were struggling against.[8] Such symbolic clashes made it all the easier for Congress to turn down the proffered reconciliation. They chose to fight on for independence and republican rule.

About a year after the Carlisle Commission returned empty-handed to London, newspapers reflected on the present state of Britain's empire in a poem called 'The Alehouse Politicians'. As the poem's speaker drank his

7 Lord Carlisle to Lady Carlisle, 4 June 1778, quoted in Brown, 'William Eden', p. 112.

8 David S. Shields and Fredrika J. Teute, 'The Meschianza: Sum of All Fêtes', *Journal of the Early Republic* 35, no. 2 (Summer 2015), pp. 185–214; Woody Holton, *Liberty Is Sweet: The Hidden History of the American Revolution* (Simon & Schuster, 2021), pp. 353–4.

morning glass of gin and warm beer, he opened his own paper to find a deluge of depressing news. Reports of bankruptcies and deaths in recent riots, plus the capture of several Caribbean sugar-islands, were 'enough to strike one dead'. Only the imminent birth of a new royal baby to the king's wife, Queen Charlotte, was taken as reason to smile. The poem ended with the speaker topping up his drink to toast both 'God Save the King' and 'the Devil take the Ministry'.[9] Such sentiments were growing almost universal as the empire staggered towards the end of the 1770s.

Disaffection was particularly acute in Britain's nearest colonial possession – Ireland. There, the expanded American war caused particularly sharp economic pain, since Irish prosperity was built substantially on its illicit trade with both the transatlantic colonies and the European continent. In the face of a potential French invasion, the imperial government in Ireland found itself too cash-strapped to raise an army, so instead a system of independent volunteer militias had sprung up in 1778. While the militias were committed to repelling an attack by Britain's Catholic enemies, they were by no means loyal servants of the British government. Rather, they proved to be the basis of renewed political struggle on the island. By the end of 1779, officials in London feared they would lose their grip on Ireland as decisively as they had lost it in America.[10]

It was not that Lord North and his government were slow to respond to the outbreak of war with France and Spain. The problem was that

9 *Bath Journal*, 18 October 1779; reprinted in the *Hibernian Chronicle*, Cork, 28 October 1779.

10 For the American Revolution's political impact in Ireland, see Neil York, 'The Impact of the American Revolution on Ireland', in H.T. Dickinson, ed., *Britain and the American Revolution* (Addison Wesley Longman, 1998), pp. 205–32; Vincent Morley, *Irish Opinion and the American Revolution, 1760–1783* (Cambridge University Press, 2002); Maurice O'Connell, *Irish Politics and Social Conflict in the Age of Revolution* (University of Pennsylvania Press, 2007); Padhraig Higgins, *A Nation of Politicians: Gender, Patriotism, and Political Culture in Late Eighteenth Century Ireland* (University of Wisconsin Press, 2010); Ultán Gillen, 'Constructing Democratic Thought in Ireland in the Age of Democratic Revolution, 1775–1800', in Joanna Innes and Mark Philp, eds, *Re-Imagining Democracy in the Age of Revolutions: America, France, Britain, Ireland 1750–1840* (Oxford University Press, 2013), pp. 149–61.

their response – extending the limited rights of Britain's Catholics, most notably by allowing them to enlist in the armed forces – made almost everything worse. Protestants throughout the empire saw this move as a highly alarming step, and not just because it weakened their religious and social supremacy. They believed, as Whig doctrine taught them, that Catholics were constitutionally indifferent to freedom. Thus, North's measure raised the spectre of a Catholic army wielded as an instrument of tyranny at home. In Scotland, opposition quickly escalated from petitions to crowd actions. According to one Edinburgh report, 'the mob . . . burnt and destroyed the houses of every Papist they could discover'.[11]

Irish resistance to Catholic relief was more restrained, not least because Catholics were a substantial majority in most communities. But it was clear the measure deepened Protestants' disgust with those in government – and thus their attachment to the rebel cause. 'In every Protestant or Dissenter's house,' the Irish-born Lord Shelburne informed Richard Price in 1779, 'the established toast is success to the Americans.'[12] Buoyed by the success of the volunteer militia, an emerging coalition of Irish merchants, tradesmen, and artisans adopted American tactics as well as rhetoric in their struggle with London. Non-importation agreements formed that year put pressure on the government to grant Ireland control of its own trade. Inspired by the Carlisle Commission, there were calls for legislative independence too. Irish people, some said, were the 'slaves' of Britain's ruling class.[13] Now was the time to push for freedom.

In November, two events helped crush the British government's resolve. First, thousands of volunteer militiamen marched through

11 Brad Jones, ' "In Favor of Popery": Patriotism, Protestantism, and the Gordon Riots in the Revolutionary British Atlantic', *Journal of British Studies* 52 (January 2013), p. 90; and see Robert Kent Donovan, 'The Military Origins of the Roman Catholic Relief Programme of 1778', *Historical Journal* 28, no. 1 (1985), pp. 79–102.

12 Lord Shelburne to Richard Price, 5 September 1779, quoted in O'Connell, *Irish Politics*, p. 124.

13 *Hibernian Journal*, Dublin, 22 December 1779, quoted in Higgins, *Nation of Politicians*, p. 247n43.

Dublin, saluting the statue of Whig hero William of Orange in a show of Protestant and anti-ministerial strength. Henry Grattan, opposition leader in the Irish parliament, proclaimed his commitment to 'revolution principles' – meaning those of John Locke and the 1688 coup against James II.[14] Then working-class Dubliners organised their own march, pouring through the streets in thousands to demonstrate outside Parliament House. While elite politicians on all sides preferred to credit the middle-class volunteer militia, it was only after workers put their bodies on the line that North relented by relaxing trade restrictions. Once again, William Eden had advised the move. Dublin's radicals, meanwhile, urged the people not to celebrate until real freedom was achieved.

When Grattan and his allies returned in the spring to push for more concessions – really, for effective Irish independence in a federal empire, much as Granville Sharp had envisaged in 1774 – the government faced a renewed dilemma. The obvious division in Irish society was that between the Protestants and Catholics. Yet anything that even looked like mobilising Catholic support risked sparking more outrage across the empire. Those in charge needed to find a different wedge with which to break the Irish challenge. What they did was target the class coalition on which – much like the cause of John Wilkes in London – the real strength of Grattan's movement rested.

Early in 1780, friends of government in Dublin began to promote an attack on journeymen's combinations – essentially, trade unions. 'These destructive combinations', wrote one critic, were 'sources of idleness, drunkenness, and cruelty'.[15] More importantly, they had forced up the wages of the city's working men. An inquiry was soon set up, and then a law proposed that promised to curb combinations and favour employers' power. Grattan raised no opposition to the measure. When a crowd of angry journeymen gathered in Phoenix Park outside Dublin that June, planning to deliver a petition to the Lord Lieutenant, it was the militia that was sent in to disperse them – a fitting symbolic gesture. By setting

---

14 Higgins, *Nation of Politicians*, p. 180.
15 O'Connell, *Irish Politics*, p. 260.

the well-to-do volunteers against their working-class neighbours, the government aimed to regain control of Irish politics. For the moment, it succeeded. Ireland stepped back from the brink of revolution.

At the same time, across the Atlantic, American patriots were confronting the contradictory potential of their own unstable revolutionary order. 'We are at this moment on a precipice,' warned the Virginian slave-trader, planter, and congressman Henry Laurens, 'and what I have long dreaded ... seems to be breaking forth – a convulsion among the people.'[16] While the Continental Army launched a devastating, genocidal campaign against Britain's Iroquois allies in western New York, the uneasy coalition between working-class and wealthy rebels was beginning to break down in the capital, Philadelphia. Having relied on American workers to begin their bid for independence four years earlier, men like Laurens turned their backs on the promise of republican equality by 1779. New types of internal conflict were the outcome.[17]

Back in 1775, when fighting first broke out between the colonists and forces of the British Empire, Pennsylvanians had formed a volunteer militia to defend themselves. Unlike the volunteers in Ireland, though, the Pennsylvania force – especially its Philadelphia units – was decidedly working class. Once the new state enshrined the militia in law,

16 Henry Laurens to John Adams, 4 October 1779; Founders Online.

17 The best account of this internal conflict is Barbara Clark Smith, *The Freedoms We Lost: Consent and Resistance in Revolutionary America* (New Press, 2010), but see also Tom Cutterham, 'Class, State, and Revolution in the History of American Capitalism', *Sociology Lens* 33, no. 1 (March 2020), pp. 26–38. For Pennsylvania, see Robert Brunhouse, *The Counter-Revolution in Pennsylvania, 1776–1790* (Pennsylvania Historical Commission, 1942); Stephen Rosswurm, *Arms, Country, and Class: The Philadelphia Militia and the 'Lower Sort' During the American Revolution, 1775–1783* (Rutgers University Press, 1987); and for Virginia, Michael McDonnell, *The Politics of War: Race, Class, and Conflict in Revolutionary Virginia* (University of North Carolina Press, 2007). For historiographies, see Richard B. Morris, 'Class Struggle and the American Revolution', *William and Mary Quarterly* 19, no. 1 (January 1962), pp. 3–29; Alfred Young and Gregory Nobles, *Whose American Revolution Was It? Historians Interpret the Founding* (New York University Press, 2011).

well-heeled citizens were forced to either volunteer their service or pay an equivalent tax: most chose to pay rather than risk fighting. Militiamen elected their own officers and organised political leadership in a Committee of Privates. These institutions, in turn, gave an armed and powerful voice to the interests of ordinary Philadelphians. A ready audience for writers like Thomas Paine, militiamen helped pressure Congress to commit to independence in 1776. Over the next few years, they exerted real influence over the life of the revolutionary city.

By 1779, though, working-class Philadelphians in and out of the militia were frustrated. Since patriots resumed control of the city the previous summer, they had found it increasingly difficult to afford the rising cost of everyday provisions. Sarah Bache, who later helped organise women for the war effort, noted that families were struggling to buy bread. War was expected to be hard, but many felt matters were worsened by merchants' selfish behaviour – when ships came in, they would buy up the goods and hold them back to keep the prices high. Bache reported how one such 'great speculator' was seized by militiamen, who paraded him around town before they 'lodged him in the Old Gaol'.[18] People thus sought to enforce fair prices in the street, and fiercely denounced those who were 'getting rich by sucking the blood of this country'.[19]

Benedict Arnold, the military governor foisted on Philadelphia after the British withdrawal, was another source of provocation to working-class citizens. He moved into a fancy townhouse and held lavish banquets, all the while scheming to profit from military contracts. His marriage in the spring of 1779 to nineteen-year-old Peggy Shippen, a prominent

---

18 John Alexander, 'The Fort Wilson Incident of 1779: A Case Study of the Revolutionary Crowd', *William and Mary Quarterly* 31, no. 4 (October 1974), p. 596. For Bache's later political life, see Emily Arendt, '"Ladies Going About for Money": Female Voluntary Associations and Civic Consciousness in the American Revolution', *Journal of the Early Republic* 34, no. 2 (Summer 2014), pp. 157–86; and Vivian Bruce Conger, 'Reading Early American Women's Political Lives: The Revolutionary Performances of Deborah Read Franklin and Sally Franklin Bache', *Early American Studies* 16, no. 2 (Spring 2018), pp. 317–52.

19 *Pennsylvania Evening Post*, 29 May 1779, quoted in Alexander, 'Fort Wilson Incident', p. 596.

merchant's daughter and one of the maidens fêted by British officers at the *meschianza* a year earlier, only sharpened the feeling that Arnold was in league with anti-revolutionary city elites. When ordinary men went off to fight, complained one militia company to the state's executive committee, they left their families 'at the mercy of the disaffected, inimical, or self-interested'. What was more, they often returned to find that such people had 'taken advantage of our absence, and enormously advanced prices on everything'.[20]

For their part, Philadelphia's financial and commercial class was also out of patience with the way the city and the state of Pennsylvania were being run. Early in 1779, they set up the so-called Republican Society aiming to organise the overthrow of the state's democratic constitution, written three years earlier. With the backing of the city's most powerful merchants, and much of its professional class too, the Republicans set about writing petitions and broadsides deriding the current constitution as inefficient. They resisted the popular price-fixing efforts however they could, publicly defending merchants' right to conduct their own business. Ultimately, their aim was to shift the blame for economic hardship away from themselves and onto the mechanisms of popular rule embedded in the constitution, the militia, and public committees.

Tensions finally exploded in October 1779, a month before the marches in Dublin that so frightened the British government. Roused by handbills calling on them to 'drive from the city all disaffected persons, and those who supported them', militiamen convened at Burn's Tavern and planned a show of force.[21] As they proceeded through the city later that day, carrying muskets and parading several prisoners, a group of some twenty Republicans convened at the home of James Wilson, a Scottish-born lawyer. When the militia were passing by, according to slightly conflicting eyewitness reports, the men in the house opened their windows and brandished weapons. Immediately, the militia reacted. In the ten-minute shoot-out that followed before the cavalry

---

20 Alexander, 'Fort Wilson Incident', p. 593.
21 Ibid., p. 601.

arrived to break it up, as many as seven men were killed – all but one of them in the street.

Following the incident, more scuffles broke out near the city jail as militiamen and others gathered to support their comrades now in custody. Arnold, the governor, claimed he was assaulted by a 'mob of lawless ruffians' and asked for a bodyguard from Congress.[22] Few Philadelphians, however, felt inclined to sympathise with him. When they went to the polls later that month, the citizens returned a new assembly majority in favour of the old, democratic constitution. Still, with blood drawn, the old coalition between working-class and wealthy patriots was decisively shattered. The 1780s would be years of mistrust and repeated efforts to squeeze popular power back out of public life. Under the pressures of war and a newfound independence, Americans' different ideas of liberty became irreconcilable.

In the closing pages of his monumental, revolutionary tract, *Political Disquisitions*, James Burgh called on the British people to form a grand association, independent of existing corrupt institutions. Only such a union, Burgh argued, could restore the principles of liberty and popular rule to the constitution. John Cartwright, another friend to the American cause, made the same call in his pamphlet, *Take Your Choice*, published in late 1776. By 1779, with government stumbling from crisis to crisis, these calls were being taken up across the country. Led by respectable men and backed by many merchants and professionals, the association movement grew in both the provinces and the metropolis. It was inspired by not only opposition writers, but also the Americans themselves, who had 'set an example before freemen of how to act when oppressed'.[23]

---

22 Benjamin Irvin, 'The Streets of Philadelphia: Crowds, Congress, and the Political Culture of Revolution, 1774–1783', *Pennsylvania Magazine of History and Biography* 129, no. 1 (January 2005), p. 38.

23 *Public Advertiser*, 2 November 1779, quoted in Micah Alpaugh, *Friends of Freedom: The Rise of Social Movements in the Age of Atlantic Revolutions* (Cambridge University Press, 2022), p. 97. For early studies of the association movement that focus on its mostly middle-class iteration in Yorkshire, see Herbert Butterfield, 'The

Petitioning was at the heart of the movement – a form of direct address from the people to their supposed representatives. Yet there were many who, like Burgh himself, recognised the insufficiency of that approach. 'Men possessed of power are not disposed to part with it', as John Jebb told assembled Middlesex associators in December 1779. They had to be moved by demonstrations of real force. The following April, Jebb and Cartwright were among those marching with a crowd of several thousand under banners reading 'Annual Parliaments and Equal Representation'. On the same day, an ally in Parliament proposed a motion designed to test support for reform. 'The influence of the crown has increased,' it declared, 'is increasing, and ought to be diminished.'[24] It was carried on a margin of eighteen votes. The establishment seemed close to giving ground.

Meanwhile that same spring, an even larger movement also sought to mobilise the power of petitioning and marches. The Protestant Association had a single unifying cause: to repeal the legislation of the year before that had loosened restrictions on the empire's Catholic population. It was led by the charismatic, twenty-nine-year-old former navy officer and Member of Parliament George Gordon (known as Lord George, because he was the younger son of a duke) – a critic of the American war, and a firm supporter of the wider movement for democratic reform. John Adams, the Massachusetts patriot who was in Europe as a diplomat, predicted Gordon would be the eighteenth century's Oliver Cromwell: the Puritan who vanquished royal power in the English Revolution of a century before.[25]

On Friday 2 June 1780, Gordon led a march of 40,000 supporters from St George's Fields – where Wilkites had been shot by soldiers twelve years earlier – to Parliament, where they presented a petition signed by more than twice as many. That same day, the Duke of Richmond in the House of Lords proposed a series of reforms straight out of the association

---

Yorkshire Association and the Crisis of 1779–80', *Transactions of the Royal Historical Society* 29 (1947), pp. 69–91; and Ian Christie, 'The Yorkshire Association, 1780–4: A Study in Political Organization', *Historical Journal* 111, no. 2 (1960), pp. 144–61.

24 Alpaugh, *Friends of Freedom*, p. 104.

25 John Adams to Edmé Jacques Genet, 20 May 1780; Founders Online. For Gordon's life, see Colin Haydon, 'Gordon, Lord George (1751–1793), Political and Religious Agitator', *Oxford Dictionary of National Biography*, 2004.

movement's programme. Boisterous crowds pushed their way into the Commons gallery to witness Parliament at work. But they were sorely disappointed when the legislators voted to delay consideration of Gordon's petition while the Lords, for their part, declined to consider Richmond's motion. That night, some vented their anger by attacking nearby Catholic chapels. Nobody, least of all Gordon himself, realised at that point that, within five days, London would be a war zone.[26]

From the beginning, rioters had different ends in mind than just attacking Catholics. While the prejudice ran deep for many, anti-popery had always also been a political attitude, rooted in ideas about power and liberty. The first night saw a police constable attacked, to shouts of 'Damn him . . . knock him on the head!' By Monday, three days later, the houses of Sir John Fielding and Lord Mansfield, the chief justice, were under attack. Far more damage was caused to these properties, bastions of the establishment approach to criminal justice, than to the chapels initially targeted – and rioters made sure that, at Bow Street, they burned Sir John's lists of suspected criminals.

On Tuesday, the riots escalated further. There were upwards of 100,000 people in the streets, a 'poor, miserable, ragged rabble' in the words of well-connected Black shopkeeper Ignatius Sancho.[27] Rioters began to target London's prisons, including the New Prison at Clerkenwell where James Aitken had once been held. They set the recently refurbished Newgate on fire, but only after they had freed its inmates. The King's Bench and Fleet prisons got the same treatment. Frances Burney, the

---

26 My account of the Gordon Riots draws especially from Hitchcock and Shoemaker, *London Lives*, pp. 343–51, as well as from George Rudé, 'The Gordon Riots: A Study of the Rioters and Their Victims', *Transactions of the Royal Historical Society* 6 (1956), pp. 93–114; Nicholas Rogers, 'Crowd and People in the Gordon Riots', in Eckhart Hellmuth, ed., *The Transformation of Political Culture: England and Germany in the Late Eighteenth Century* (Oxford University Press, 1990), pp. 39–55; Ian Haywood and John Seed, eds, *The Gordon Riots: Politics, Culture and Insurrection in Late Eighteenth-Century Britain* (Cambridge University Press, 2012); Matthew Lockwood, *To Begin the World Over Again: How the American Revolution Devastated the Globe* (Yale University Press, 2019), pp. 65–9; Alpaugh, *Friends of Freedom*, pp. 105–9. For the transatlantic politics of the riots, see Lauren Michalak, ' "The Mobs All Cryd Peace with America": The Gordon Riots and Revolution in England and America" (PhD diss., University of Maryland, 2023).

27 Lockwood, *To Begin the World Over Again*, p. 65.

novelist, witnessed 'flames ascending from Newgate' as well as from 'Justice Fielding's house' at Bow Street.[28] It was as if the whole of London were ablaze, and the established order had at last collapsed upon itself. 'This, this is liberty,' reflected Sancho bitterly, 'genuine British liberty!'

London's criminal justice regime was one thing, but the rioters did not stop there. Their anger engulfed the entire edifice of Britain's imperial power. Targeted buildings included the slave-trading South Sea Company, the East India Company, and the Navy Pay Office. Many in the crowd were sailors with first-hand experience of British discipline and warfare overseas. Others were Black refugees who had escaped America during the war.[29] By Wednesday, with the prisons already in flames, the riot reached the peak of its ferocity. The crowd attacked what was perhaps the true centre of Britain's empire – the Bank of England. It was at this point that John Wilkes, the city alderman and one-time leader of the London crowd, entered the fray. He manned the barricades in defence of the Bank, shooting two rioters dead outside the gates.[30]

Many, like Wilkes, who opposed the riot, also wished to see it ended without royal troops being deployed. Middle-class Londoners banded together to protect their property, including as members of volunteer militias – but magistrates refused to call in professional soldiers against the city's people.[31] In the end, the government sent in the troops without permission, ordering them to open fire without first reading the Riot Act as law demanded. Lord Mansfield provided the threadbare legal justification, claiming each man simply acted in his capacity as a citizen. Hundreds of rioters were killed as 15,000 soldiers swarmed the city. The rebellion was crushed within a day, and London left a smoking, bloody

28 Hitchcock and Shoemaker, *London Lives*, p. 349.

29 For Black rioters, see ibid., p. 345; Peter Linebaugh and Marcus Rediker, *The Many-Headed Hydra: Sailors, Slaves, Commoners and the Hidden History of the Revolutionary Atlantic* (Verso, 2000), p. 288.

30 Hitchcock and Shoemaker, *London Lives*, p. 350; Robin Eagles, *Champion of English Freedom: The Life of John Wilkes, MP and Lord Mayor of London* (Amberley Publishing, 2024), pp. 214–18.

31 For the role of volunteer militia against and alongside professional soldiers, see Matthew McCormack, 'Supporting the Civil Power: Citizen Soldiers and the Gordon Riots', *London Journal* 37, no. 1 (2012), pp. 27–41.

ruin. Gordon, who had tried to halt the violence, was arrested on the charge of treason and imprisoned in the Tower of London.

In the aftermath, government kept its troops on high alert around the city. Twenty-six rioters were eventually hanged – thirty-six more had death sentences commuted. Rather than make any concessions to the demands of the wider reform movement, and its supporters on both sides of the riot, the government chose to call elections under the old, corrupt, deeply inequitable rules. With arm-twisting and bribery, they managed to secure a new majority, fit for another seven years of rule. The outcome disgusted and dismayed members of the reform associations. For others, it simply confirmed the British constitution's true nature. As one correspondent to a London paper put it that December, 'a committee of the people with muskets in their hands and spirit in their hearts are the only means to redress public grievances.'[32]

Newgate Prison set ablaze during the Gordon
Riots, 1780 (British Museum)

---

32 *Public Ledger*, 16 December 1780, quoted in Alpaugh, *Friends of Freedom*, p. 108.

Lord North may have won his new majority in late 1780, but he scarcely had time to enjoy it. News of the catastrophe at Yorktown in October 1781 – with the main bulk of the British Army in America captured by a joint French–Continental force – finally gave George III no choice but to accept his resignation. When North's rival, the Marquess of Rockingham, took office in March 1782, one of his first acts was to initiate peace negotiations with the American diplomats in Paris. Having spent the past eight years warning about the devastation that war with the colonists would cause to the strength and dignity of Britain's empire, Rockingham's Whigs now had to deal with the complex, messy aftermath.

In Ireland, the change of ministry opened the gates to a renewed political struggle. Even before Rockingham took office, thousands of militia volunteers began convening in Dungannon, County Tyrone, to prepare a programme of demands. 'The spirit of liberty is abroad,' they declared, 'embraced by the people at large, and every day brings with it an accession of strength.'[33] Henry Grattan welcomed the renewal of the old cross-class alliance as the Dublin workers once more rallied to his cause. Dungannon's representative in Ireland's parliament – none other than William Eden, now chief secretary of Ireland – told colleagues that he 'would not answer for the consequences' if demands for legislative independence were not met.[34] Rockingham listened, and, within a month, repealed the laws subordinating Dublin legislators to their London counterparts.

Across the Atlantic, the approaching rebel triumph brought crucial dilemmas of freedom into sharper focus. For Indigenous people across North America, the peace was a disaster that lay the groundwork for a century of further conquest. Betrayed by their former British allies, most Native Americans east of the Mississippi experienced the outcome of the war as a substantial weakening of independence and geopolitical leverage.[35] Black patriots, meanwhile, mustered strategic optimism that

---

33 Alpaugh, *Friends of Freedom*, p. 137.

34 Ibid., p. 138.

35 For the impact of the 1783 Treaty of Paris on Indigenous peoples, see Colin Calloway, 'Suspicion and Self-Interest: The British–Indian Alliance and the Peace of Paris', *Historian* 48, no. 1 (1985), pp. 41–60; Alan Taylor, *The Divided Ground: Indians,*

the moment had come for the end of slavery. 'My virtuous fellow citizens,' pleaded a self-styled Black Whig in 1782, 'after you have rid yourselves of the British yoke', surely the next step would be to 'emancipate those who have been all their life subject to bondage'.[36] In New England, slavery was already being dismantled by Black people themselves. Might a wider contagion of liberty at last be possible?[37]

The truth was that, for most enslaved people, the best route to freedom ran through the invading British Army. After Lord Dunmore's offer of freedom to fighting-age Black men in Virginia in 1775, and a widening of that promise throughout the rebel colonies in 1779, tens of thousands of those enslaved by white patriots fled to the British lines. Henry

---

Settlers, and the Northern Borderlands of the American Revolution (Alfred A. Knopf, 2006), esp. pp. 111–12; Jeffrey Ostler, *Surviving Genocide: Native Nations and the United States from the American Revolution to Bleeding Kansas* (Yale University Press, 2019), pp. 74–5; and Kathleen DuVal, *Independence Lost: Lives on the Edge of the American Revolution* (Random House, 2015), esp. pp. 229–38. On the problems of sovereignty and international law that emerged from the peace, see Gregory Ablavsky, 'Species of Sovereignty: Native Nationhood, the United States, and International Law, 1783–1795', *Journal of American History* 106, no. 3 (December 2019), pp. 591–613.

36 Manisha Sinha, *The Slave's Cause: A History of Abolition* (Yale University Press, 2016), p. 46.

37 In addition to Sinha, *The Slave's Cause*, there is an extensive literature on slavery and emancipation struggles in the era of the American Revolution: see Benjamin Quarles, *The Negro in the American Revolution* (University of North Carolina Press, 1996 [1961]); David Brion Davis, *The Problem of Slavery in the Age of Revolution, 1770–1823* (Cornell University Press, 1975); Gary Nash, *Race and Revolution* (Madison House, 1990); Sylvia Frey, *Water from the Rock: Black Resistance in a Revolutionary Age* (Princeton University Press, 1991); Douglas Egerton, *Death or Liberty: African Americans and Revolutionary America* (Oxford University Press, 2009); David Waldstreicher, *Slavery's Constitution: From Revolution to Ratification* (Farrar, Straus & Giroux, 2009); Christopher Leslie Brown, 'The Problems of Slavery', in Edward Gray and Jane Kamensky, eds, *The Oxford Handbook of the American Revolution* (Oxford University Press, 2015), pp. 427–46. For New England, see John Wood Sweet, 'More than Tears: The Ordeal of Abolition in Revolutionary New England', *Explorations in Early American Culture* 5 (2001), pp. 118–72; Chernoh Sesay Jr, 'The Revolutionary Black Roots of Slavery's Abolition in Massachusetts', *New England Quarterly* 87, no. 1 (2014), pp. 99–131; Gloria McCahon Whiting, 'Emancipation Without the Courts or Constitution: The Case of Revolutionary Massachusetts', *Slavery and Abolition* 41, no. 3 (2020), pp. 458–78.

Washington, who escaped from George Washington's plantation at Mount Vernon, shipped out with the British as they evacuated Charleston at the end of 1782. He joined Boston King, a carpenter from South Carolina, in the British colony of Nova Scotia. There, these men and their wives, along with several thousand other freedom seekers, tried to forge new lives among the sometimes-hostile white settlers.[38] United States diplomats, meanwhile, fought to have these escapees restored to their enslavers – or at least to have the British pay them compensation.

Black colonists did fight alongside Continentals in the war, too. Many, such as Lemuel Haynes from Connecticut, went on to be outspoken abolitionists. But their service did not translate into a politics of practical anti-slavery among the majority of white patriots. In 1783, the white Quaker David Cooper wrote *A Serious Address to the Rulers of the United States* that ended up on George Washington's bookshelf. Cooper mourned the fact that although 'few among us are now hardy enough to justify slavery', still almost no one would 'release their slaves'. The victory just won turned out to have been for 'the *rights* of *white men*', he wrote, 'not *all men*'.[39] If Washington read the pamphlet, he did little to embrace its sentiments. Nor did most of his fellow founders.

Just because the British helped free thousands in the war, of course, did not make theirs an empire of liberty. For most Black people around the globe, the empire remained as much a 'low abyss of tyranny and despotism' as any other colonial European power.[40] Its policy towards American slavery was, for the most part, based on pragmatism – and it fought hard to preserve its Caribbean colonies. Benjamin Whitecuff, a free Black farmer from Long Island, served as a British spy until he was captured by rebels. Having escaped a death sentence and rejoined British

38 Cassandra Pybus, *Epic Journeys of Freedom: Runaway Slaves of the American Revolution and Their Global Quest for Liberty* (Beacon Press, 2006), pp. 41–2, 59–60, 213, 218. See also Simon Schama, *Rough Crossings: Britain, the Slaves, and the American Revolution* (BBC Books, 2005).

39 Sinha, *Slave's Cause*, p. 39; see François Furstenberg, 'Atlantic Slavery, Atlantic Freedom: George Washington, Slavery, and Transatlantic Abolitionist Networks', *William and Mary Quarterly* 28, no. 2 (April 2011), pp. 247–86.

40 Sinha, *Slave's Cause*, p. 46.

service, he ended up at the siege of Gibraltar, one of the war's last major battles. When Whitecuff finally made it to England, he claimed £130 compensation for the property he had left behind in America. The commissioners awarded him £10.[41]

Rockingham's Whig government might just, perhaps, have followed through on its promise to pursue the parliamentary reforms demanded by the national association movement. But the death of Rockingham himself a few months after he took office threw the British ruling class into another bout of brutal internecine struggle. His successor, Lord Shelburne – a friend and patron of dissenting intellectuals like Richard Price – barely had time to negotiate a peace treaty before he was ousted by former ally Charles Fox in a wildly unexpected coalition with Lord North. The war finally over, Britain's imperial crisis ebbed away – and, with it, the leverage that had advanced the cause of liberty and popular rule over the past twenty years. Yet within another decade, the French Revolution would renew the sense of crisis tenfold. With it, a new generation of working-class saboteurs and traitors were to take up arms against the empire.

41 Pybus, *Epic Journeys*, p. 79.

Conclusion

Part of the paradox of British liberty in the eighteenth century was this: freedom was founded in the right to revolution, yet defending it meant granting loyalty to the imperial state. In the wars with France and Spain that filled the century, the same wars that drove the expansion of the empire's destructive and oppressive power at great cost to millions of working people, most British subjects understood their nation as a champion of civil and religious liberty. The American Revolution presented a dilemma because it drove a wedge between the splendour of the empire and the theory of freedom that supposedly underpinned it. Those who most warmly took the rebels' side insisted that the empire could be re-made, with the Americans inside it, and restored to its true purpose in the world.

Once the War of Independence turned into another war with France and Spain in 1778, a version of British imperial loyalty could all too easily reassert itself. 'The mob all cried peace with America, and war with France,' the diplomat John Adams reported to his wife Abigail after the Gordon Riots in 1780; 'poor wretches! As if this were possible.'[1] Without admitting it, government policy reflected this popular attitude

---

1 John Adams to Abigail Adams, 17 June 1780; Founders Online.

– British leaders shifted their resources from the theatre of mainland North America towards the Caribbean, where the struggle with rival slaveholding empires was fought. James Aitken's campaign of sabotage did not directly shape this policy, but it did add bite to the threat posed by the rebels' friends at home. British strategy responded to questions of loyalty on both sides of the Atlantic. Aitken's treason was a part of that.

After the war, British advocates of the American cause framed the outcome less as a blow to Britain's empire than as a victory for shared notions of freedom. For the Welsh dissenter Richard Price whose work had helped inspire Aitken, it was a 'revolution in favour of universal liberty' that had opened 'a new prospect in human affairs'. It would benefit Britons most of all, provided they could 'catch the flame of virtuous liberty which has favoured their American brethren'. At the same time, Price did not absolve the new nation of its responsibility as an emergent champion of liberty. 'Nothing can excuse the United States', he wrote in 1785, if the people held in slavery there were not freed as soon as possible.[2]

When the people of France rose against their rulers four years later, the British revolutionary tradition faced another challenge. Should events in France be understood as a continuation of the spread of universal liberty, or as an aberration that threatened to upset the social order throughout Europe? Some who had been allies of the American colonies nonetheless took the latter view – most notably, former Bristol MP Edmund Burke. Yet men like Price welcomed the onset of revolution in France. In a much-read 1789 address to the Revolution Society, he placed the French tumult within the lineage of Britain's 1688 and denounced the spirit of rivalry between nations. If government in France became a force for liberty rather than despotism, Price thought, then it would cease to be Britain's enemy.

Against Price's optimism, however, stood the power and self-interest of the British ruling class. His death in 1791 spared him from seeing how things turned out. What really transformed the situation was the

2 Richard Price, *Observations on the Importance of the American Revolution* (London, 1785), pp. 1, 47.

revolution's escalation from a constitutional coup to a full-blown popular revolt, reaching its pinnacle in 1793 with the execution of the king and the formation of a French republic. France's ruling National Convention then declared war with Britain and the other European monarchies, whom it accused – rightly – of plotting to restore the monarchy. Once more, events had cut a line between the strength of Britain's empire and the politics of freedom. This time, though, the threat of a Catholic French monarchy could not be used to counteract domestic disaffection. For those who sympathised with French republicans, it was now Britain's empire that posed the greatest threat to liberty around the globe.

These reversals help explain the extraordinary steps the British government took in the 1790s to repress political dissent. Of course, even those measures – banning meetings and dissenting publications, prosecuting political opponents for treason, and empowering authorities to hold suspects indefinitely without charge – were defended by the men who instituted them as temporary sacrifices, 'by which the blessings of liberty may be transmitted to our children unimpaired'.[3] John Cartwright, with decades of experience since his first sallies against constitutional corruption in the 1770s, thought differently. Writing to his wife Anne, he called it 'a system of proscription and terror'.[4] The government's frantic hunt for a conspiracy of arsonists in the early months of 1777 turned out to be something of a dress rehearsal for the nationwide clampdown it undertook in the 1790s.

All across the British Empire, the French Revolution helped spark uprisings, conspiracies, and new visions of liberty – especially among the working class. Thomas Hardy, a shoemaker from the Scottish Lowlands, was one of the founders of a revolutionary organisation, the London Corresponding Society. Other members included Thomas Paine, the poet and engraver William Blake, and the Black abolitionist Olaudah Equiano. Hardy's life was remarkably like Aitken's: his father died when

---

3 William Wilberforce, quoted in Clive Emsley, 'Repression, "Terror" and the Rule of Law in England During the French Revolution', *English Historical Review* 100 (October 1985), p. 804.

4 John Cartwright to Anne Cartwright, quoted in Emsley, 'Repression', p. 810.

he was eight, and he moved down to London just before the outbreak of the American war. Both men were born in 1752, which made Hardy forty-four when he was put on trial by the British government for treason. Unlike Aitken, though, Hardy won his acquittal. After the trial, he returned to his shoe-shop and lived to the age of eighty.[5]

Edward Despard, born in Ireland one year before Aitken and Hardy, lived an even more adventurous life. The youngest of eight children, he learned the classics at a Quaker school and joined the British Army at the age of fifteen – as an officer, the thing Aitken had once longed for. Posted to Jamaica, Despard fought the Spanish in the American war and served in Belize after the peace. Somewhere in that time, he married Catherine, a free Black woman who went with him to England in 1790. Radicalised by his experience on the imperial front line, Despard joined both the London Corresponding Society and the United Irishmen, whose own uprising was defeated in 1798. Despard's story ends in 1803 with his execution for treason. He and his comrades, the authorities claimed, planned to occupy the Bank of England and assassinate the king.[6]

Or consider Richard Parker, a younger man who lived a little longer than Aitken did. A baker's son, Parker apprenticed as a navigator at the age of twelve and went to sea with the navy at fifteen. But, as a junior officer in his mid-twenties, he started resisting orders and was stripped of his rank. Desperately short of money after three years on shore, Parker re-enlisted as a seaman early in 1797. He was twenty-nine and married,

5 Thomas Hardy, *Memoir of Thomas Hardy, Founder of and Secretary to the London Corresponding Society* (London, 1832); and see E.P. Thompson, *The Making of the English Working Class* (Penguin, 2013 [1963]), pp. 19–22.

6 Peter Linebaugh and Marcus Rediker, *The Many-Headed Hydra: Sailors, Slaves, Commoners and the Hidden History of the Revolutionary Atlantic* (Verso, 2000), pp. 248–86; Mike Jay, *The Unfortunate Colonel Despard* (Bantam Press, 2004); Peter Linebaugh, *Red Round Globe Hot Burning: A Tale at the Crossroads of Commons and Closure, of Love and Terror, of Race and Class, and of Kate and Ned Despard* (University of California Press, 2021). See more generally Ian McCalman, *Radical Underworld: Prophets, Revolutionaries, and Pornographers in London, 1795–1840* (Oxford University Press, 1993); Michael T. Davis and Paul A. Pickering, eds, *Unrespectable Radicals: Popular Politics in the Age of Reform* (Ashgate, 2008).

with two infant sons. That May, as mutiny swept across the British fleets anchored at Spithead and the Nore, he became the president of the 'floating republic' at the mouth of the Thames. When the mutiny collapsed weeks later, Parker was executed on the deck of the ninety-gun warship, *Sandwich* – crowds came to the London dockside to honour Parker's body, rescued from desecration by his wife, Ann.[7]

Britain's eighteenth-century revolutionaries never matched the achievements of their American, French, or Haitian counterparts. They did not overthrow the regime that oppressed them or establish new forms of republican rule. But they did help to shape the broader age of revolutions, contributing to a great movement for liberty that went beyond the boundaries of any one country or empire. They helped forge a tradition of working-class consciousness and emancipatory politics that carried on into the nineteenth century and beyond. More than just making the English working class, though, they were part of an Atlantic and even a global freedom movement. Even as race, gender, capital, and empire fractured that movement from its outset, there remained threads of connection that stem from a basic, shared insistence upon liberty.[8]

Acts of rebellion and sabotage have not, of course, been unique to the age of revolution. As the weapons of the weak against the strong, they have occurred wherever power was abused, people exploited and oppressed, justice distorted and withheld. Long before and long after the late eighteenth century, enslaved people rose up and burned down their tyrants' houses – or, like many other workers, they engaged in subtler

---

7 Ann Veronica Coats, 'Parker, Richard (1767–1797), Seaman and Mutineer', *Oxford Dictionary of National Biography*, 2004; Niklas Frykman, *The Bloody Flag: Mutiny in the Age of Atlantic Revolution* (University of California Press, 2020), pp. 155–7.

8 For scholarship that emphasises the transnational nature of the age of revolution, see Linebaugh and Rediker, *Many-Headed Hydra*; Janet Polasky, *Revolutions Without Borders: The Call to Liberty in the Atlantic World* (Yale University Press, 2015); Micah Alpaugh, *Friends of Freedom: The Rise of Social Movements in the Age of Atlantic Revolutions* (Cambridge University Press, 2022). For a critique of the liberal transnational perspective as 'history writing for neoliberal times', see Sarah Knott, 'Narrating the Age of Revolution', *William and Mary Quarterly* 73, no. 1 (January 2016), pp. 3–36, quotation at p. 21.

forms of sabotage, including feigned incompetence and accidents or simply slower, less efficient work.[9] Weavers in Spitalfields began to slash work from the looms of those who undercut their wages in the decade before Aitken came to London. Later, Luddites smashed the looms themselves, and wrecked machines of all descriptions in their struggle to hold power over their own working lives.[10]

When Ruby Montoya and Jessica Reznicek used welding torches to destroy valves on the oil pipeline meant to run from shale fields in North Dakota to a terminal in Illinois in 2016, they intensified a campaign of resistance that was led by members of the Standing Rock Sioux tribe. Protesters established roadblocks and disrupted the construction of the pipeline, fearing its impact on local water sources – as well as its contribution to the burning of fossil fuels that threatens ecosystems and human survival all over the planet. The home-made incendiary devices that Montoya and Reznicek used to set heavy construction machinery on fire bore a resemblance to those Aitken deployed more than two centuries before. Their actions prevented the combustion of an estimated 30 million barrels of oil. Reznicek was sentenced to eight years in prison.[11]

Since 2020, a British activist group called Palestine Action has conducted a sabotage campaign against the manufacturers of weapons used by the Israeli military in Palestine. Rather than fire, their tactics often involved the use of blood-red paint meant to symbolise the

9 See Michael Craton, *Testing the Chains: Resistance to Slavery in the British West Indies* (Cornell University Press, 1982); James Oakes, 'The Political Significance of Slave Resistance', *History Workshop Journal* 22, no. 1 (Autumn 1986), pp. 89–107; Stephanie Camp, *Closer to Freedom: Enslaved Women and Everyday Resistance in the Plantation South* (University of North Carolina Press, 2004). On the category of 'resistance' in slavery scholarship, see Walter Johnson, 'On Agency', *Journal of Social History* 37, no. 1 (Fall 2003), pp. 113–24.

10 Eric Hobsbawm, 'The Machine Breakers', *Past and Present* 1 (February 1952), pp. 57–70. For a present-oriented analysis, see Gavin Mueller, *Breaking Things at Work: The Luddites Were Right About Why You Hate Your Job* (Verso, 2021).

11 Julia Shipley, 'You Strike a Match', *Rolling Stone*, 26 May 2021. Situating Montoya and Reznicek in the politics of climate sabotage and the ethics of non-violence, see Andreas Malm, *How to Blow Up a Pipeline* (Verso, 2021), esp. pp. 97–100, 107; Dylan Manson, 'Eco-Sabotage as Defensive Activism', *Ethical Theory and Moral Practice* 27 (May 2024), pp. 505–22.

suffering and death caused by deployment of the weapons themselves. In the summer of 2025, more than a year into an escalating genocide conducted by the government of Israel in Gaza, the group sprayed red paint in the engines of two Royal Air Force planes at an airbase in Oxfordshire. Soon afterwards, the British government declared the group a terrorist organisation. Men and women who held placards saying 'I oppose genocide, I support Palestine Action' were arrested and imprisoned under terror laws. Meanwhile, security was stepped up at Britain's airbases.[12]

In the United States, a country born in revolution, the meaning of liberty and what it means to struggle for it have often been narrowed and distorted to a point that few if any revolutionaries would have recognised. Historians work to recover what was lost or buried, what has fallen out of common stories that we tell ourselves about the past – or, indeed, stories that were never told, or not to those who needed to hear. This book tells a story of the American Revolution that sits awkwardly alongside celebrations of the founding fathers. At the same time, it is not a book that says we would be better off without the revolution. It reminds us that we all have revolutionary heritage. Even a person with no obvious advantages – that is, any ordinary one of us – could strike a blow that brings freedom for all a little closer. So, at least, believed the revolutionaries of 1780 when they urged one another to remember James Aitken. They took courage from the thought, and perhaps we can too.

12 Chris Mason and Zahra Fatima, 'Palestine Action to Be Banned After RAF Base Break In', BBC News, 20 June 2025; Doug Faulkner, 'Arrests at Rally Against Palestine Action Ban Rise to 890', BBC News, 7 September 2025.

Acknowledgements

If James Aitken had help from friends or fellow revolutionaries during his sabotage mission – other than from Silas Deane, safely in Paris – he never revealed the secret. Fortunately, I need not take any such precautions to protect those who assisted the writing of this book.

At the University of Birmingham, I have the privilege to work with a remarkable group of American historians who are also engaged citizens and activists. Their inspiration, conversation, and encouragement have been vital to this project. Thanks, Nathan Cardon, Steve Hewitt, La Shonda Mims, and John Munro – and John especially, for his detailed attention to the manuscript while I was still finishing writing it. I have also gained enormously from the wisdom, advice, and support of many other Birmingham colleagues, in particular Karen Harvey, a fellow explorer of the eighteenth century. In some ways, the spirit of this book was nurtured on UCU picket lines over the last decade. I am grateful to all the dear colleagues who were there with me.

However tenuous and compromised it may be, the historical profession continues to function as a republic of letters, sustaining conviviality and intellectual collaboration across all sorts of boundaries. I am deeply indebted to Patrick Griffin, Frank Cogliano, Woody Holton, and Eliga Gould, both for their scholarship and for their generous friendship. This book also benefited from the many conversations that have been facilitated by the AHRC-sponsored Reframing the Age of Revolutions project; thanks to Peter Hill, Juan Neves-Sarriegui, Andrew Edwards, and Felicia Gottmann, as well as all who took part in the project's events.

Cameron Kline gave crucial advice on parts of the manuscript. Henry Snow graciously shared their work in progress on Atlantic dockside labour regimes. Nick Guyatt saw the potential of a book like this long before I did. John Wyatt Greenlee drew the maps brilliantly. Jessica Warner, whose own biography of Aitken still contains the most detailed account of his life, responded generously to my emails, sharing references from her surviving notes. At Verso, I am immensely grateful to Seb Budgen for making the book happen, and to Melissa Weiss, Jeanne Tao, and everyone else involved in putting it together.

Finally, thanks to my mum, Tina, whose disputatious spirit has something in common with James Aitken's; to my long-suffering, beloved partner, Jessica Johnson, without whose patience, strength, and good humour this book would not exist; and to my son, Joseph, whose contribution has been altogether immeasurable and nothing less than essential.

Index